MW01635895

BEST EVER

MEDITERRANEAN

A COLLECTION OF OVER **100** ESSENTIAL RECIPES

This edition published in 2011
LOVE FOOD is an imprint of Parragon Books Ltd

Parragon
Queen Street House
4 Queen Street
Bath BA1 1HE, UK

Copyright © Parragon Books Ltd 2006

LOVE FOOD and the accompanying heart device is a registered trademark of Parragon Books Ltd in Australia, the UK, USA, India, and the EU.

All rights reserved. No part of this publication may be reproduced, stored in a retrieval system, or transmitted, in any form or by any means, electronic, mechanical, photocopying, recording, or otherwise, without the prior permission of the copyright holder.

ISBN: 978-1-4454-4367-6

Printed in China

Designed by Terry Jeavons & Company

Notes for the Reader
This book uses imperial, metric, and US cup measurements. Follow the same units of measurement throughout; do not mix imperial and metric. All spoon measurements are level: teaspoons are assumed to be 5 ml, and tablespoons are assumed to be 15 ml. Unless otherwise stated, milk is assumed to be whole, eggs and individual vegetables such as potatoes are medium, and pepper is freshly ground black pepper.

The times given are an approximate guide only. Preparation times differ according to the techniques used by different people and the cooking times may also vary from those given as a result of the type of oven used. Optional ingredients, variations or serving suggestions have not been included in the calculations.

Recipes using raw or very lightly cooked eggs should be avoided by infants, the elderly, pregnant women, convalescents, and anyone with a chronic condition. Pregnant and breastfeeding women are advised to avoid eating peanuts and peanut products. Sufferers from nut allergies should be aware that some of the ready-prepared ingredients used in the recipes in this book may contain nuts. Always check the packaging before use.

Picture Acknowledgements
The publisher would like to thank the following for permission to reproduce copyright material on the front cover: Vegetable tajine©Simon Brown/Getty Images

MEDITERRANEAN

introduction

The Mediterranean Sea is part of the Atlantic Ocean and covers a huge area almost completely enclosed by land, with Europe to the north, Africa to the south, and Asia to the east. Countries bordering the sea include Spain, France, Italy, Greece, Turkey, Lebanon, Egypt, Tunisia, and Morocco.

The many positive health aspects of what has come to be known as 'the Mediterranean diet' have been widely recognized in recent years. The warm, sunny climate and miles of coastal waters enjoyed by the Mediterranean countries provide a diet that is rich in seafood, with only limited amounts of meat and dairy products, and a stunning range of colorful, nutrition-packed fruits and vegetables. Plenty of olive oil, with its heart-protective properties, completes the picture of a way of eating that promotes an enviably long and healthy life.

The Mediterranean diet is not only healthy, however—it is also absolutely delicious! Although the countries that border this vast sea share many ingredients in common—eggplants, zucchini, tomatoes, garlic, onions, and fresh herbs, as well as pork, lamb, beef, chicken, and an incredible variety of seafood—each country has its own characteristic way of transforming these ingredients into wonderful dishes that taste of sunshine. Perhaps the most popular and well-known cuisines are those of Spain, France, Italy, and Greece, but most cultures will include versions of the same, very simple, dishes in their repertoire, such as fish, broiled or grilled with lemon and herbs, or roast lamb with garlic.

Whether your aim is to enjoy the health benefits of the Mediterranean diet or simply to discover more about the fabulous cuisine of this part of the world, remember to use top-quality ingredients, grown locally if possible, and to allow plenty of time to relax over your meal!

soups & appetizers

Eating in countries around the Mediterranean is a leisurely, sociable affair, and meals often start with a selection of appetizers, such as the Spanish tapas, or the Greek and Middle Eastern meze, to linger and chat over.

Olives are a simple and very typical way to start—they are served throughout the area, and are perfect with a glass of chilled sherry or white wine, so keep a bottle of Cracked Marinated Olives in the refrigerator to dip into. Chickpeas form the basis for a tasty Tunisian soup, a delicious dip, and Falafel, crisp little balls flavored with garlic and spices. Eggplants are used in several countries to make an irresistible dip—Baba Ghanoush is the Middle Eastern specialty.

Fish, as you might expect, makes frequent appearances as an appetizer. It is often cooked in batter—Calamari, deep-fried squid, is served in most seaside restaurants. Monkfish, Rosemary, & Bacon Skewers and White Fish & Caper Croquettes are popular Spanish tapas, and Boreks are filo pastries from Turkey, filled here with tuna and tomato.

Stuffed Vine Leaves are a feature of a Greek meze, while Artichokes with Vièrge Sauce and Asparagus with Hollandaise Sauce are elegant appetizers, typical of French cuisine!

chilled cucumber soup

ingredients

SERVES 4

2 medium cucumbers

10 fl oz/300 ml/$1^1/_4$ cups strained plain yogurt

10 fl oz/300 ml/$1^1/_4$ cups chicken stock

2 tbsp walnut oil

1 large garlic clove, crushed

3 tbsp chopped fresh dill

salt and pepper

4 oz/115 g/1 cup walnut pieces, chopped

method

1 Peel the cucumbers and chop the flesh into small dice. Beat the yogurt with the chicken stock, the walnut oil, garlic, and dill, reserving a little to garnish. Stir in the chopped cucumber and season with salt and pepper.

2 Chill the soup in the refrigerator for at least 4 hours.

3 Stir in the chopped walnuts and serve garnished with the reserved chopped dill.

vegetable & bean soup

ingredients

SERVES 4–6

8 oz/225 g fresh fava beans
2 tbsp olive oil
2 large garlic cloves, crushed
1 large onion, finely chopped
1 celery stalk, finely chopped
1 carrot, peeled and chopped
6 oz/175 g firm new potatoes, diced
24 fl oz/940 ml/3¾ cups vegetable stock
2 beefsteak tomatoes, peeled, seeded, and chopped
salt and pepper
1 large bunch of fresh basil, tied with kitchen string
7 oz/200 g zucchini, diced
7 oz/200 g green beans, trimmed and chopped
2 oz/55 g dried vermicelli, broken into pieces, or small pasta shapes

pistou sauce

3½ oz/100 g fresh basil leaves
2 large garlic cloves
1½ tbsp pine nuts
scant ¼ cup fruity extra-virgin olive oil
½ cup finely grated Parmesan cheese

method

1 If the fava beans are very young and tender, they can be used as they are. If they are older, use a small, sharp knife to slit the gray outer skins, then ‘pop’ out the green beans.

2 Heat the olive oil in a large heavy-bottom pan, over medium heat. Add the garlic, onion, celery, and carrot, and sauté until the onion is soft, but not brown.

3 Add the potatoes, stock, and tomatoes, and season with salt and pepper. Bring to a boil, skimming the surface if necessary, then add the basil. Reduce the heat and cover the pan. Let simmer for 15 minutes, or until the potatoes are tender.

4 Meanwhile, make the pistou sauce. Whiz the basil, garlic, and pine nuts in a food processor or blender until a thick paste forms. Add the extra-virgin olive oil and whiz again. Transfer to a bowl and stir in the cheese, then cover and chill until required.

5 When the potatoes are tender, stir the fava beans, zucchini, green beans, and vermicelli into the soup and continue simmering for 10 minutes, or until the vegetables are tender and the pasta is cooked. Taste, and adjust the seasoning if necessary. Remove and discard the bunch of basil.

6 Ladle the soup into bowls and add a spoonful of pistou sauce to each bowl.

bouillabaisse

ingredients

SERVES 4

- $3^1/_2$ fl oz/100 ml/scant $^1/_2$ cup olive oil
- 3 garlic cloves, chopped
- 2 onions, chopped
- 2 tomatoes, seeded and chopped
- 22 fl oz/700 ml/generous $2^3/_4$ cups fish stock
- 14 fl oz/400 ml/$1^3/_4$ cups white wine
- 1 bay leaf
- pinch of saffron threads
- 2 tbsp chopped fresh basil
- 2 tbsp chopped fresh parsley
- 7 oz/200 g live mussels
- 9 oz/250 g snapper or monkfish fillets
- 9 oz/250 g haddock fillets, skinned
- 7 oz/200 g shrimp, shelled and deveined
- $3^1/_2$ oz/100 g scallops
- salt and pepper
- fresh baguettes, to serve

method

1 Heat the oil in a large pan over medium heat. Add the garlic and onions and cook, stirring, for 3 minutes. Stir in the tomatoes, stock, wine, bay leaf, saffron, and herbs. Bring to a boil, reduce the heat, cover, and simmer for 30 minutes.

2 Meanwhile, soak the mussels in lightly salted water for 10 minutes. Scrub the shells under cold running water and pull off any beards. Discard any with broken shells. Tap the remaining mussels and discard any that refuse to close. Put the rest into a large pan with a little water, bring to a boil and cook over high heat for 4 minutes. Remove from the heat and discard any that remain closed.

3 When the tomato mixture is cooked, rinse the fish, pat dry, and cut into chunks. Add to the pan and simmer for 5 minutes. Add the mussels, shrimp, and scallops, and season. Cook for 3 minutes, until the fish is cooked through. Remove from the heat, discard the bay leaf, and ladle into serving bowls. Serve with fresh baguettes.

tunisian garlic & chickpea soup

ingredients

SERVES 4

8 tbsp olive oil
12 garlic cloves, very finely chopped
12 oz/350 g/2 cups dried chickpeas, soaked overnight in cold water and drained
40 fl oz/2.5 liters/ $10^1/_2$ cups water
1 tsp ground cumin
1 tsp ground coriander
2 carrots, very finely chopped
2 onions, very finely chopped
6 celery stalks, very finely chopped
juice of 1 lemon
salt and pepper
4 tbsp chopped fresh cilantro

method

1 Heat half the oil in a large, heavy-bottom pan. Add the garlic and cook over low heat, stirring frequently, for 2 minutes. Add the chickpeas to the pan with the measured water, cumin, and ground coriander. Bring to a boil, then reduce the heat and let simmer for $2^1/_2$ hours, or until tender.

2 Meanwhile, heat the remaining oil in a separate pan. Add the carrots, onions, and celery. Cover and cook over medium-low heat, stirring occasionally, for 20 minutes.

3 Stir the vegetable mixture into the pan of chickpeas. Transfer about half the soup to a food processor or blender and process until smooth. Return the purée to the pan, add about half the lemon juice, and stir. Taste and add more lemon juice as required. Season with salt and pepper. Ladle into warmed bowls, sprinkle with the fresh cilantro, and serve.

cracked marinated olives

ingredients

SERVES 8

1 lb/450 g can or jar unpitted large green olives, drained
4 garlic cloves, peeled
2 tsp coriander seeds
1 small lemon
4 sprigs of fresh thyme
4 feathery stalks of fennel
2 small fresh red chiles (optional)
pepper
Spanish extra-virgin olive oil, to cover

method

1 To allow the flavors of the marinade to penetrate the olives, place on a cutting board and, using a rolling pin, bash them lightly so that they crack slightly. Alternatively, use a sharp knife to cut a lengthwise slit in each olive as far as the pit. Using the flat side of a broad knife, lightly crush each garlic clove. Using a mortar and pestle, crack the coriander seeds. Cut the lemon, with its rind, into small chunks.

2 Put the olives, garlic, coriander seeds, lemon chunks, thyme sprigs, fennel, and chiles, if using, in a large bowl and toss together. Season with pepper to taste, but you should not need to add salt as preserved olives are usually salty enough. Pack the ingredients tightly into a glass jar with a lid. Pour in enough olive oil to cover the olives, then seal the jar tightly.

3 Let the olives stand at room temperature for 24 hours, then marinate in the refrigerator for at least a week, but preferably 2 weeks, before serving. From time to time, gently give the jar a shake to remix the ingredients. Return the olives to room temperature and remove from the oil to serve. Provide toothpicks for spearing the olives.

tapenade

ingredients

MAKES ABOUT 10 1/2 OZ/300 G

9 oz/250 g black olives, such as Nyons or Niçoise, pitted
3 anchovy fillets in oil, drained
1 large garlic clove, halved, with the green center removed, if necessary
2 tbsp pine nuts
1/2 tbsp capers in brine, rinsed
4 fl oz/125 ml/1/2 cup extra-virgin olive oil
freshly squeezed lemon or orange juice, to taste
pepper

garlic croûtes

12 slices French bread, about 1/4 inch/5 mm thick
extra-virgin olive oil
2 garlic cloves, peeled and halved

method

1 Put the olives, anchovy fillets, garlic, pine nuts, and capers in a food processor or blender and whiz until well blended. With the motor still running, pour the olive oil through the feed tube and continue blending until a loose paste forms.

2 Add the lemon juice and pepper to taste. It shouldn't need any salt because of the saltiness of the anchovies. Cover and chill until required.

3 To make the garlic croûtes, preheat the broiler to high. Place the bread slices on the broiler rack and toast 1 side for 1–2 minutes, or until golden brown. Flip the bread slices over, lightly brush the untoasted side with olive oil, then toast for 1–2 minutes.

4 Rub 1 side of each bread slice with the garlic cloves while it is still hot, then set aside and let cool completely. Store in an airtight container for up to 2 days.

5 Serve the tapenade with the garlic croûtes.

hummus dip

ingredients

SERVES 4

- 115 g/4 oz/scant 3/4 cup dried chickpeas
- 3–6 tbsp lemon juice
- 3–6 tbsp water
- 2–3 garlic cloves, crushed
- 5 fl oz/150 ml/2/3 cup sesame seed paste
- salt
- 1 tbsp olive oil
- 1 tsp cayenne pepper or paprika
- 1 fresh flat-leaf parsley sprig, to garnish
- pita bread, fresh salad greens, and slices of fresh tomato, to serve

method

1 Soak the chickpeas overnight in enough cold water to cover them and allow room for expansion. Drain the chickpeas, place them in a pan, cover with fresh cold water, bring to a boil, then let boil for about 1 hour, or until tender. Remove from the heat and drain.

2 Place the chickpeas in a food processor and blend with enough lemon juice and water to make a thick, smooth paste.

3 Add the garlic cloves and mix well. Add the sesame seed paste and salt to taste. Add more lemon juice or water, if necessary, to get the flavor and consistency that you want.

4 Spoon into a serving dish, drizzle over the oil, and sprinkle with either cayenne pepper or paprika.

5 Cover with plastic wrap and chill for at least 1 hour before serving. Garnish with a fresh parsley sprig and serve with pita bread, fresh salad greens, and slices of tomato.

baba ghanoush with flat breads

ingredients

SERVES 4–6

1 large eggplant, pricked all over with a fork
3 fat garlic cloves, unpeeled
1 tsp ground coriander
1 tsp ground cumin
1 tbsp light sesame seed paste
juice of 1/2 lemon
2 tbsp extra-virgin olive oil
salt and pepper
fresh cilantro, to garnish

flat breads

9 oz/250 g/scant 2 cups white bread flour
2 tbsp fine cornmeal
1 tsp baking powder
1 tsp salt
scant 4 tbsp butter, diced
1 tbsp sesame seeds (optional)
5–6 fl oz/150–175 ml/ 2/3–3/4 cup warm water
corn oil, for oiling

method

1 Bake the eggplant in a roasting pan in a preheated oven, 400°F/200°C, for 25 minutes. Add the garlic cloves and cook for 15 minutes until the eggplant and garlic are very tender.

2 Halve the eggplant and scoop the flesh into a food processor. Peel the garlic cloves and add to the eggplant with the spices, sesame seed paste, lemon juice, and oil. Process until smooth, then season to taste. Transfer to a serving dish, garnish, and cover until required.

3 To make the flat breads, sift the flour, cornmeal, baking powder, and salt into a mixing bowl, then rub in the butter until the mixture resembles bread crumbs. Add the sesame seeds, if using, and stir in the water, first with a wooden spoon, then with your hands to bring the mixture together into a ball.

4 Turn the mixture out onto a lightly floured counter and knead lightly until a soft dough forms. Divide into 6 pieces, then roll each into a ball. Wrap in plastic wrap and let rest in the refrigerator for 30 minutes.

5 Roll out or press the dough balls with your fingers into 1/4-inch/5-mm-thick circles. Heat a lightly oiled grill pan over medium heat and cook for a few minutes on each side until lightly golden. Serve warm with the dip.

falafel

ingredients

SERVES 4

225 g/8 oz/1 1/3 cups dried chickpeas
1 large onion, finely chopped
1 garlic clove, crushed
salt and cayenne pepper
2 tbsp chopped fresh parsley
2 tsp ground cumin
2 tsp ground coriander
1/2 tsp baking powder
vegetable oil, for deep-frying
hummus dip (see page 20) and pita bread, to serve

method

1 Soak the chickpeas overnight in enough cold water to cover them and allow room for expansion. Drain the chickpeas, place them in a pan, cover with fresh cold water, bring to a boil, then let boil for about 1 hour, or until tender. Remove from the heat and drain.

2 Place the chickpeas in a food processor and process to make a coarse paste. Add the onion, garlic, seasoning, parsley, spices, and baking powder and process again to mix.

3 Let the mixture rest for 30 minutes, then divide into 8 equal pieces. Shape each piece into a ball between the palms of your hands and arrange on a plate. Let rest for a further 30 minutes.

4 Heat the oil for deep-frying in a wok or deep pan. Gently drop in the balls and cook until golden brown. Carefully remove from the oil and drain for a few minutes on a plate lined with paper towels.

5 Serve the falafel hot or at room temperature accompanied with hummus dip and pita bread.

chicken in lemon & garlic

ingredients

SERVES 6–8

4 large skinless, boneless chicken breasts
5 tbsp Spanish olive oil
1 onion, finely chopped
6 garlic cloves, finely chopped
grated rind of 1 lemon, finely pared rind of 1 lemon and juice of both lemons
4 tbsp chopped fresh flat-leaf parsley, plus extra to garnish
salt and pepper
lemon wedges and crusty bread, to serve

method

1 Using a sharp knife, slice the chicken breasts widthwise into very thin slices. Heat the olive oil in a large, heavy-bottom skillet, add the onion and cook for 5 minutes, or until softened, but not browned. Add the garlic and cook for an additional 30 seconds.

2 Add the sliced chicken to the skillet and cook gently for 5–10 minutes, stirring from time to time, until all the ingredients are lightly browned and the chicken is tender.

3 Add the grated lemon rind and the lemon juice and let it bubble. At the same time, deglaze the skillet by scraping and stirring all the bits on the bottom of the skillet into the juices with a wooden spoon. Remove the skillet from the heat, stir in the parsley, and season with salt and pepper.

4 Transfer the chicken in lemon and garlic, piping hot, to a warmed serving dish. Sprinkle with the pared lemon rind, garnish with the parsley, and serve with lemon wedges for squeezing over the chicken, accompanied by chunks or slices of crusty bread for mopping up the lemon and garlic juices.

monkfish, rosemary, & bacon skewers

ingredients

SERVES 4–6

9 oz/250 g monkfish fillet
12 stalks of fresh rosemary
3 tbsp Spanish olive oil
juice of 1/2 small lemon
1 garlic clove, crushed
salt and pepper
6 thick slices Canadian bacon
lemon wedges, to garnish
garlic mayonnaise, to serve

method

1 Slice the monkfish fillets in half lengthwise, then cut each fillet into 12 bite-size chunks to make a total of 24 pieces. Put the monkfish pieces in a large bowl.

2 To prepare the rosemary skewers, strip the leaves off the stalks and set them aside, leaving a few leaves at one end.

3 For the marinade, finely chop the reserved leaves and whisk together in a bowl with the olive oil, lemon juice, garlic, salt, and pepper. Add the monkfish pieces and toss until coated in the marinade. Cover and let marinate in the refrigerator for 1–2 hours.

4 Cut each bacon slice in half lengthwise, then in half widthwise, and roll up each piece. Thread 2 pieces of monkfish alternately with 2 bacon rolls onto each rosemary skewer.

5 Preheat the broiler, grill pan, or barbecue. If you are cooking the skewers under a broiler, arrange them on the broiler pan so that the leaves of the rosemary skewers protrude from the broiler and do not catch fire. Broil the monkfish and bacon skewers for 10 minutes, turning from time to time and basting with any remaining marinade, or until cooked. Serve hot, garnished with lemon wedges, with a bowl of garlic mayonnaise, for dipping.

white fish & caper croquettes

ingredients

MAKES 12

- 12 oz/350 g white fish fillets, such as cod, haddock, or monkfish, skinned and boned
- 10 fl oz/300 ml/1 1/4 cups milk
- salt and pepper
- 2 oz/55 g butter
- 2 oz/55 g/scant 1/2 cup all-purpose flour
- 4 tbsp capers, coarsely chopped
- 1 tsp paprika
- 1 garlic clove, crushed
- 1 tsp lemon juice
- 3 tbsp chopped fresh flat-leaf parsley, plus extra sprigs to garnish
- 1 egg, beaten
- 2 oz/55 g/1 cup fresh white bread crumbs
- 1 tbsp sesame seeds
- corn oil, for deep-frying
- lemon wedges, to garnish
- mayonnaise, to serve

method

1 Put the fish fillets and milk in a large skillet and season to taste. Bring to a boil, then lower the heat, cover the skillet, and cook for 8–10 minutes, or until the fish flakes easily. Remove the fish, reserving the milk. Flake the fish.

2 Heat the butter in a pan. Stir in the flour and cook gently, stirring, for 1 minute. Gradually stir in the reserved milk until smooth. Slowly bring to a boil, stirring, until the sauce thickens.

3 Remove from the heat, add the flaked fish, and beat until smooth. Add the capers, paprika, garlic, lemon juice, and parsley and mix well. Season to taste. Transfer to a dish and let cool. Cover and chill for 2–3 hours.

4 Pour the beaten egg onto a plate. Combine the bread crumbs and sesame seeds on a separate plate. Divide the fish mixture into 12 portions and form each portion into a 3-inch/7.5-cm sausage shape. Dip each croquette in the beaten egg, then coat it in the bread crumb mixture. Let chill for 1 hour.

5 Heat the oil in a deep-fryer to 350–375°F/180–190°C. Cook the croquettes, in batches, for 3 minutes, or until golden brown and crispy. Drain well on paper towels. Serve garnished with lemon wedges and parsley sprigs, with a bowl of mayonnaise for dipping.

tuna & tomato boreks

ingredients

MAKES 18

about 18 sheets filo pastry, 15 x 6 inches/38 x 15 cm each, thawed if frozen
vegetable oil, for sealing and pan-frying
sea salt, to garnish
green salad and lemon wedges, to serve

filling

2 hard-cooked eggs, shelled and finely chopped
7 oz/200 g canned tuna in brine, drained
1 tbsp chopped fresh dill
1 tomato, peeled, seeded, and very finely chopped
1/4 tsp cayenne pepper
salt and pepper

method

1 To make the filling, put the eggs in a bowl with the tuna and dill and mash the mixture until blended.

2 Stir in the tomato, taking care not to break it up too much. Season with the cayenne pepper salt, and pepper. Set aside.

3 Lay a sheet of filo pastry out on a counter with a short side nearest to you, keeping the remaining sheets covered with a damp dish towel. Arrange about 1 tablespoon of the filling in a line along the short side, about 1/2 inch/ 1 cm in from the end and 1 inch/2.5 cm in from both long sides.

4 Make one tight roll to enclose the filling, then fold in both long sides for the length of the filo. Continue rolling up to the end. Use a little vegetable oil to seal the end. Repeat to make 17 more rolls, or until all the filling has been used up.

5 Heat 1 inch/2.5 cm of oil in a skillet to 350–375°F/180–190°C, or until a cube of bread browns in 30 seconds. Deep-fry 2–3 boreks at a time for 2–3 minutes until golden brown. Remove with a slotted spoon and drain well on paper towels. Sprinkle with sea salt. Serve hot or at room temperature with a green salad and lemon wedges for squeezing over.

calamari

ingredients

SERVES 6

1 lb/450 g prepared squid
all-purpose flour, for coating
sunflower-seed oil, for deep-frying
salt
lemon wedges, to garnish
garlic mayonnaise, to serve

method

1 Slice the squid into 1/2-inch/1-cm rings and halve the tentacles if large. Rinse under cold running water and dry well with paper towels. Dust the squid rings with flour so that they are lightly coated.

2 Heat the oil in a deep-fat fryer, large, heavy-bottom pan, or wok to 350–375°F/180–190°C, or until a cube of bread browns in 30 seconds. Deep-fry the squid rings in small batches for 2–3 minutes, or until golden brown and crisp all over, turning several times (if you deep-fry too many squid rings at one time, the oil temperature will drop and they will be soggy). Do not overcook as the squid will become tough and rubbery rather than moist and tender.

3 Remove with a slotted spoon and drain well on paper towels. Keep warm in a low oven while you deep-fry the remaining squid rings.

4 Sprinkle the fried squid rings with salt and serve piping hot, garnished with lemon wedges for squeezing over. Accompany with a bowl of garlic mayonnaise for dipping.

mussels with herb & garlic butter

ingredients

SERVES 8

1 lb 12 oz/800 g live mussels
splash of dry white wine
1 bay leaf
6 tbsp butter
$1^3/_4$ oz/35 g/generous $^1/_2$ cup fresh white or brown bread crumbs
4 tbsp chopped fresh flat-leaf parsley, plus extra sprigs to garnish
2 tbsp snipped fresh chives
2 garlic cloves, finely chopped
salt and pepper
lemon wedges, to serve

method

1 Clean the mussels by scrubbing or scraping the shells and pulling out any beards that are attached to them. Discard any with broken shells and any that refuse to close when tapped. Put the mussels in a colander and rinse well under cold running water.

2 Put the mussels in a large pan and add the wine and bay leaf. Cook, covered, over high heat, shaking the pan occasionally, for 3–4 minutes, or until the mussels have opened. Discard any mussels that remain closed. Drain the mussels.

3 Shell the mussels, reserving one half of each shell. Arrange the mussels, in their half shells, in a large, shallow, ovenproof serving dish.

4 Melt the butter in a small pan and pour into a small bowl. Add the bread crumbs, parsley, chives, garlic, salt, and pepper and mix together well. Leave until the butter has set slightly. Using your fingers or 2 teaspoons, take a large pinch of the butter mixture and use to fill each mussel shell, pressing it down well.

5 Bake the mussels in a preheated oven, 450°F/230°C, for 10 minutes, or until hot. Serve at once, garnished with parsley sprigs, and accompanied by lemon wedges for squeezing over.

lime-drizzled shrimp

ingredients

SERVES 6

4 limes
12 raw jumbo shrimp, in their shells
3 tbsp Spanish olive oil
2 garlic cloves, finely chopped
splash of fino sherry
salt and pepper
4 tbsp chopped fresh flat-leaf parsley

method

1 Grate the rind and squeeze the juice from 2 of the limes. Cut the remaining 2 limes into wedges and set aside for later.

2 To prepare the shrimp, remove the head and legs, leaving the shells and tails intact. Using a sharp knife, make a shallow slit along the back of each shrimp, then pull out the dark vein and discard. Rinse the shrimp under cold water and dry on paper towels.

3 Heat the olive oil in a large, heavy-bottom skillet, then add the garlic and cook for 30 seconds. Add the shrimp and cook for 5 minutes, stirring from time to time, or until they turn pink and start to curl. Mix in the lime rind, juice, and a splash of sherry to moisten, then stir well together.

4 Transfer the cooked shrimp to a serving dish, season with salt and pepper, and sprinkle with the parsley. Serve piping hot, accompanied by the reserved lime wedges for squeezing over the shrimp.

scallops with bread crumbs & parsley

ingredients

SERVES 4

- 20 large fresh scallops, shucked, about $1^1/_2$ inches/4 cm thick
- salt and pepper
- 7 oz/200 g clarified butter
- 3 oz/85 g day-old French bread, made into fine bread crumbs
- 4 garlic cloves, finely chopped
- 5 tbsp finely chopped fresh flat-leaf parsley
- lemon wedges, to serve

method

1 Preheat the oven to its lowest temperature. Use a small knife to remove the dark vein that runs around each scallop, then rinse and pat dry. Season with salt and pepper and set aside.

2 Melt half the butter in a large sauté pan or skillet over high heat. Add the bread crumbs and garlic, then reduce the heat to medium and cook, stirring, for 5–6 minutes, or until the bread crumbs are golden brown and crisp. Remove the bread crumbs from the pan and drain well on paper towels, then keep warm in the oven. Wipe out the pan.

3 Use 2 large sauté pans or skillets to cook all the scallops at once without overcrowding the pans. Melt scant 2 oz/55 g of the butter in each pan over high heat. Reduce the heat to medium. Divide the scallops between the 2 pans in single layers; cook for 2 minutes.

4 Turn the scallops over and continue pan-frying for an additional 2–3 minutes, or until they are golden and cooked through if you cut one with a knife. Add extra butter to the pans if necessary.

5 Divide the scallops among 4 warmed plates and sprinkle with the bread crumbs and parsley mixed together. Serve with lemon wedges for squeezing over.

stuffed vine leaves

ingredients

MAKES ABOUT 30

8-oz/225-g package vine leaves preserved in brine
4 oz/115 g/$^{2}/_{3}$ cup Arborio or other short-grain rice
6 fl oz/175ml/$^{3}/_{4}$ cup olive oil
1 small onion, chopped finely
1 garlic clove, chopped finely
2 oz/55 g/$^{1}/_{3}$ cup pine nuts, chopped
2 oz/55 g/$^{1}/_{3}$ cup currants
3 scallions, chopped finely
1 tbsp chopped fresh mint
1 tbsp chopped fresh dill
2 tbsp chopped fresh flat-leaf parsley
salt and pepper
juice of 1 lemon
lemon wedges and strained plain yogurt, to serve

method

1 Place the vine leaves in a bowl, add boiling water, and soak for 20 minutes. Drain, soak in cold water for 20 minutes, and drain again.

2 Meanwhile, cover the rice with cold water in a pan, bring to the boil, then simmer for 15–20 minutes, or until tender. Drain well and set aside in a bowl to cool.

3 Heat 2 tablespoons of the oil in a skillet and fry the onion and garlic until softened. Add to the rice with the pine nuts, currants, scallions, mint, dill, and parsley. Season with a little salt and plenty of pepper, and mix together well.

4 Place one vine leaf, vein-side upward, on a counter. Put a little filling on the base of the leaf and fold up the bottom end of the leaf. Fold in the sides, then roll up the leaf around the filling. Squeeze gently to seal. Fill and roll the remaining leaves, then pack the stuffed leaves close together in a large flameproof casserole, seam-side down and in a single layer.

5 Mix the remaining oil and the lemon juice with 5 fl oz/150 ml/$^{2}/_{3}$ cup water and pour into the casserole. Place a large plate over the vine leaves to keep them in place then cover the casserole with a lid. Bring to simmering point, then simmer for 45 minutes. Leave the vine leaves to cool in the liquid.

6 Serve warm or chilled, with lemon wedges and yogurt.

artichokes with vièrge sauce

ingredients

SERVES 4

4 large globe artichokes
1/2 lemon, sliced
salt

vièrge sauce

3 large beefsteak tomatoes, peeled and seeded, then finely diced
4 scallions, very finely chopped
6 tbsp chopped fresh herbs, such as basil, chervil, chives, mint, flat-leaf parsley, or tarragon
5 fl oz/150 ml/2/3 cup full-flavored extra-virgin olive oil
pinch of sugar
salt and pepper

method

1 To prepare the artichokes, cut off the stems and trim the bottom so that it will stand upright on the plate. Use scissors to snip the leaf tips off each artichoke, then drop in a large bowl of water with 2 of the lemon slices while the others are being prepared.

2 Meanwhile, select a pan large enough to hold all 4 artichokes upright and half-fill with salted water and the remaining lemon slices. Bring the water to a boil, then add the artichokes and place a heatproof plate on top to keep them submerged. Reduce the heat to a low boil and continue boiling the artichokes for 25–35 minutes, depending on their size, until the bottom leaves pull out easily.

3 While the artichokes are cooking, prepare the vièrge sauce. Put the tomatoes, scallions, herbs, oil, sugar, salt, and pepper in a pan and set aside for the flavors to blend.

4 When the artichokes are tender, drain them upside-down on paper towels, then transfer to individual plates. Heat the sauce very gently until it is just warm, then spoon it equally over the artichokes.

asparagus with hollandaise sauce

ingredients

SERVES 4

1 lb 7 oz/650 g green asparagus, with any woody ends broken off and the stalks trimmed to the same height

hollandaise sauce

4 tbsp white wine vinegar
1/2 tbsp finely chopped shallot
5 black peppercorns
1 bay leaf
3 large egg yolks
5 oz/140 g unsalted butter, finely diced
2 tsp lemon juice
salt
pinch of cayenne pepper

method

1 Divide the asparagus into 4 bundles and tie each with kitchen string, criss-crossing the string from just below the tips to the base. Stand the bundles upright in a deep pan. Add boiling water to come three-quarters of the way up the stalks, then cover with a loose tent of foil, shiny-side down, inside the pan. Heat the water until bubbles appear around the side of the pan, then let simmer for 10 minutes, or until the stalks are just tender when pierced with the tip of a knife. Drain well.

2 Meanwhile, to make the hollandaise sauce, boil the vinegar, shallot, peppercorns, and bay leaf in a pan over high heat until reduced to 1 tablespoon. Let cool slightly, then strain into a heatproof bowl that will fit over a pan of simmering water without touching the water.

3 Beat the egg yolks into the bowl. Set the bowl over the pan of simmering water and whisk the egg yolks constantly until they are thick enough to leave a trail on the surface. Do not let the water boil. Gradually beat in the butter, piece by piece, whisking constantly until the sauce is like soft mayonnaise. Stir in the lemon juice, then add salt to taste and the cayenne pepper. Serve immediately with the asparagus.

Route de Fontainebleau
Tél:01 64 98 85 97

sicilian stuffed tomatoes

ingredients

SERVES 4

8 large, ripe tomatoes
7 tbsp extra-virgin olive oil
2 onions, finely chopped
2 garlic cloves, crushed
4 oz/115 g/2 cups fresh bread crumbs
8 anchovy fillets in oil, drained and chopped
3 tbsp black olives, pitted and chopped
2 tbsp chopped fresh flat-leaf parsley
1 tbsp chopped fresh oregano
4 tbsp freshly grated Parmesan cheese

method

1 Cut a thin slice off the tops of the tomatoes and discard. Scoop out the seeds with a teaspoon and discard, taking care not to pierce the shells. Turn the tomato shells upside down on paper towels to drain.

2 Heat 6 tablespoons of the olive oil in a skillet, add the onions and garlic, and cook over low heat, stirring occasionally, for 5 minutes, until softened. Remove the skillet from the heat and stir in the bread crumbs, anchovies, olives, and herbs.

3 Using a teaspoon, fill the tomato shells with the bread crumb mixture, then place in an ovenproof dish large enough to hold them in a single layer. Sprinkle the tops with grated Parmesan and drizzle with the remaining oil.

4 Bake in a preheated oven, 350°F/180°C, for 20–25 minutes, until the tomatoes are tender and the topping is golden brown.

5 Remove the dish from the oven and serve immediately, if serving hot, or let cool to room temperature.

stuffed pimientos

ingredients

MAKES 7–8

$6\frac{1}{2}$ oz/185 g bottled whole pimientos del piquillo

fillings

curd cheese & herb

8 oz/225 g/1 cup curd cheese
1 tsp lemon juice
1 garlic clove, crushed
4 tbsp chopped fresh flat-leaf parsley
1 tbsp chopped fresh mint
1 tbsp chopped fresh oregano
salt and pepper

tuna mayonnaise

7 oz/200 g canned tuna steak in olive oil, drained
5 tbsp mayonnaise
2 tsp lemon juice
2 tbsp chopped fresh flat-leaf parsley
salt and pepper

goat cheese & olive

$1\frac{3}{4}$ oz/50 g pitted black olives, finely chopped
7 oz/200 g soft goat cheese
1 garlic clove, crushed
salt and pepper

method

1 Lift the peppers from the jar, reserving the oil for later.

2 To make the curd cheese and herb filling, put the curd cheese in a bowl and add the lemon juice, garlic, parsley, mint, and oregano. Mix well together. Season to taste with salt and pepper.

3 To make the tuna mayonnaise filling, put the tuna in a bowl and add the mayonnaise, lemon juice, and parsley. Add 1 tablespoon of the reserved oil from the jar of pimientos and mix well. Season with salt and pepper.

4 To make the goat cheese and olive filling, put the olives in a bowl, and add the goat cheese, garlic, and 1 tablespoon of the reserved oil from the jar of pimientos. Mix well together. Season with salt and pepper.

5 Using a teaspoon, heap the filling of your choice into each pimiento. Put in the refrigerator and let chill for at least 2 hours until firm.

6 To serve the pimientos, arrange them on a serving plate and, if necessary, wipe with paper towels to remove any of the filling that has spread over the skins.

meat & poultry

Meat is enjoyed in all Mediterranean countries, although not necessarily in great quantities. Roast lamb is a particular favorite, served on festive occasions such as Easter, and marries well with the herb rosemary, which grows wild and profusely. Try Roast Lamb with Rosemary & Marsala for the Italian twist—the pan juices are reduced to a thick, syrupy, delicious sauce to serve with the lamb. In Morocco, lamb is served as a 'tagine,' an unusual dish cooked with vegetables and apricots, which is low in fat, high in flavor, and excellent served with couscous.

Meat is often transformed into sausages—try Sausages with Lentils, a Spanish dish that uses spicy lamb or beef merguez sausages, but which can also be made with pork or wild boar sausages. Chickens are raised in all Mediterranean countries, and are often free-range, so have an excellent flavor. In Greece, where chickens are often seen happily foraging on country roadsides, they are used in a pie with crisp, flaky filo pastry, and Chicken Kabobs with Yogurt Sauce are served in most Greek tavernas. In France, Chicken in Tarragon Sauce is a classic dish—the sauce is rich, creamy, and flavorful.

Paella is a specialty of Spain that combines chicken with seafood, especially shrimp. This is definitely a treat to try!

roast lamb with rosemary & marsala

ingredients

SERVES 6

4 lb/1.8 kg leg of lamb
2 garlic cloves, sliced thinly
2 tbsp rosemary leaves
8 tbsp olive oil
salt and pepper
2 lb/900 g potatoes, cut into 1-inch/2.5-cm cubes
6 fresh sage leaves, chopped
4 fl oz/150 ml/2/3 cup Marsala

method

1 Use a small, sharp knife to make incisions all over the lamb, opening them out slightly to make little pockets. Insert the garlic slices and about half the rosemary leaves in the pockets.

2 Place the lamb in a roasting pan and spoon half the olive oil over it. Roast in a preheated oven, 425°F/220°C, for 15 minutes. Reduce the oven temperature to 350°F/180°C. Remove the lamb from the oven, and season to taste. Turn the lamb over, return to the oven, and roast for an additional hour.

3 Meanwhile, spread out the cubed potatoes in a second roasting pan, pour the remaining olive oil over them, and toss to coat. Sprinkle with the remaining rosemary and the sage. Place the potatoes in the oven with the lamb, and roast for 40 minutes.

4 Remove the lamb from the oven, turn it over, and pour over the Marsala. Return it to the oven with the potatoes, and cook for an additional 15 minutes.

5 Transfer the lamb to a carving board and cover with foil. Place the roasting pan over high heat, bring the juices to a boil, and let boil until thickened and syrupy, then strain. Carve the lamb into slices and serve with the potatoes and sauce.

provençal barbecued lamb

ingredients

SERVES 4–6

1 leg of lamb, about 3 lb 5 oz/1.5 kg, boned
olive oil, for brushing

marinade

1 bottle full-bodied red wine
2 large garlic cloves, chopped
2 tbsp extra-virgin olive oil
large handful of fresh rosemary sprigs, plus extra to garnish
fresh thyme sprigs, plus extra to garnish

black olive tapenade

9 oz/250 g/1 1/2 cups black olives in brine, rinsed and pitted
1 large garlic clove
2 tbsp walnut pieces
4 canned anchovy fillets, drained
4 fl oz/125 ml/1/2 cup extra-virgin olive oil
lemon juice, to taste
pepper

method

1 Place the lamb on a cutting board. Holding the knife almost flat, slice horizontally into the pocket left by the leg bone, taking care not to cut all the way through, so the meat can be opened out flat. Place in a large nonmetallic bowl and add the marinade ingredients. Cover with plastic wrap and let marinate in the refrigerator for 24 hours, turning several times.

2 To make the tapenade, blend the olives, garlic, walnut pieces, and anchovies in a food processor. With the motor running, slowly add the olive oil through the feed tube. Add lemon juice and pepper to taste. Transfer to a bowl, cover and let chill until required.

3 Remove the lamb from the marinade and pat dry. Lay the lamb flat and thread 2–3 long metal skewers through the flesh, so that the meat remains flat while it cooks. Spread the tapenade all over the lamb on both sides.

4 Brush the grill rack with oil. Place the lamb on the rack about 4 inches/10 cm above hot coals and cook for 5 minutes. Turn and cook for an additional 5 minutes. Turn twice more at 5-minute intervals. Raise the rack if the meat begins to look charred—it should be medium-cooked after 20–25 minutes.

5 Remove the lamb from the heat and let stand for 10 minutes. Carve into thin slices and garnish with rosemary and thyme sprigs.

marinated lamb & vegetable kabobs

ingredients

SERVES 4

juice of 2 large lemons
$3^1/_2$ fl oz/100 ml/generous $^1/_3$ cup olive oil, plus extra for oiling
1 garlic clove, crushed
1 tbsp chopped fresh oregano or mint
salt and pepper
1 lb 9 oz/700 g boned leg or fillet of lamb, trimmed and cut into $1^1/_2$-inch/4-cm cubes
2 green bell peppers
2 zucchini
12 pearl onions, peeled and left whole
8 large bay leaves
lemon wedges, to garnish
rice, to serve

cucumber and yogurt dip

1 small cucumber
10 fl oz/300 ml/$1^1/_4$ cups strained plain yogurt
1 large garlic clove, crushed
1 tbsp chopped fresh mint or dill
salt and pepper

method

1 To make the cucumber and yogurt dip, peel then coarsely grate the cucumber. Put in a strainer and squeeze out as much of the water as possible. Put the cucumber into a bowl. Add the yogurt, garlic, and chopped mint, season with pepper and mix thoroughly. Let chill in the refrigerator for 2 hours. Sprinkle with salt just before serving.

2 Put the lemon juice, oil, garlic, oregano or mint, salt, and pepper in a bowl and whisk together. Add the lamb to the marinade.

3 Toss the lamb in the marinade, cover and refrigerate overnight or for at least 8 hours. Stir occasionally to coat the lamb.

4 When ready to serve, core and seed the bell peppers, and cut into $1^1/_2$-inch/4-cm pieces. Cut the zucchini into 1-inch/2.5-cm pieces. Thread the lamb, bell peppers, zucchini, onions, and bay leaves onto 8 flat, oiled metal kabob skewers, alternating and dividing the ingredients as evenly as possible. Place on an oiled broiler pan.

5 Cook the kabobs under a preheated broiler for 10–15 minutes, turning frequently and basting with any remaining marinade. Serve hot, garnished with lemon wedges, with rice and the cucumber and yogurt dip.

lamb with balsamic & rosemary marinade

ingredients

SERVES 6

6 racks of lamb, each with 3 chops

fresh rosemary sprigs, to garnish

marinade

3 tbsp chopped fresh rosemary

1 small onion, finely chopped

3 tbsp olive oil

1 tbsp balsamic vinegar

1 tbsp lemon juice

salt and pepper

method

1 Put the lamb in a large, shallow dish and sprinkle with the chopped rosemary and onion. Whisk together the olive oil, balsamic vinegar, and lemon juice and season with salt and pepper.

2 Pour the balsamic mixture over the lamb, turning well to coat. Cover with plastic wrap and set aside in a cool place to marinate for 1–2 hours.

3 Drain the lamb, reserving the marinade. Grill the racks over hot coals, brushing frequently with the reserved marinade, for 8–10 minutes on each side. Serve garnished with rosemary sprigs.

tagine of lamb

ingredients

SERVES 4

1 tbsp sunflower or corn oil
1 onion, chopped
12 oz/350 g boneless lamb, trimmed of all visible fat and cut into 1-inch/2.5-cm cubes
1 garlic clove, finely chopped
20 fl oz/625 ml/2½ cups vegetable stock
grated rind and juice of 1 orange
1 tsp clear honey
1 cinnamon stick
½-inch/1-cm piece fresh gingerroot, finely chopped
1 eggplant
4 tomatoes, peeled and chopped
4 oz/115 g/⅔ cup no-soak dried apricots
2 tbsp chopped fresh cilantro
salt and pepper
freshly cooked couscous, to serve

method

1 Heat the oil in a large, heavy-bottom skillet or ovenproof casserole over medium heat. Add the onion and lamb cubes and cook, stirring frequently, for 5 minutes, or until the meat is lightly browned all over. Add the garlic, stock, orange rind and juice, honey, cinnamon stick, and ginger. Bring to a boil, then reduce the heat, cover, and let simmer for 45 minutes.

2 Using a sharp knife, halve the eggplant lengthwise and slice thinly. Add to the skillet with the chopped tomatoes and apricots. Cover, and cook for an additional 45 minutes, or until the lamb is tender.

3 Stir in the cilantro and season with salt and pepper. Serve immediately, straight from the skillet, with freshly cooked couscous.

lamb with tomatoes, artichokes, & olives

ingredients

SERVES 4

- 4 tbsp strained plain yogurt
- grated rind of 1 lemon
- 2 garlic cloves, crushed
- 3 tbsp olive oil
- 1 tsp ground cumin
- salt and pepper
- 1 lb 10 oz/700 g lean boneless lamb, cubed
- 1 onion, sliced thinly
- 5 fl oz/150 ml/2/3 cup dry white wine
- 1 lb/450 g tomatoes, chopped coarsely
- 1 tbsp tomato paste
- pinch of sugar
- 2 tbsp chopped fresh oregano or 1 tsp dried
- 2 bay leaves
- 3 oz/85g/1/2 cup kalamata olives
- 14 oz/400 g canned artichoke hearts, drained and halved

method

1 Put the yogurt, lemon rind, garlic, 1 tablespoon of the olive oil, cumin, salt, and pepper in a large bowl and mix together. Add the lamb and toss together until coated in the mixture. Cover and let marinate for at least 1 hour.

2 Heat 1 tablespoon of the olive oil in a large flameproof casserole. Add the lamb in batches and fry for about 5 minutes, stirring frequently, until browned on all sides. Using a slotted spoon, remove the meat from the casserole and set aside. Add the remaining tablespoon of oil to the casserole with the onion and fry for 5 minutes, until softened.

3 Pour the wine into the casserole, stirring in any glazed bits from the bottom, and bring to a boil. Reduce the heat and return the meat to the casserole, then stir in the tomatoes, tomato paste, sugar, oregano, and bay leaves.

4 Cover the casserole with a lid and simmer for about 1 1/2 hours, until the lamb is tender. Stir in the olives and artichokes and simmer for another 10 minutes. Serve hot.

moussaka

ingredients

SERVES 4

2 eggplants, thinly sliced
1 lb/450 g fresh lean ground beef
2 onions, thinly sliced
1 tsp finely chopped garlic
14 oz/400 g canned tomatoes
2 tbsp chopped fresh parsley
salt and pepper
2 eggs
10 fl oz/300 ml/1 1/4 cups strained plain yogurt
1 tbsp freshly grated Parmesan cheese

method

1 Dry-fry the eggplant slices, in batches, in a nonstick skillet on both sides until browned. Remove from the skillet.

2 Add the beef to the skillet and cook for 5 minutes, stirring, until browned. Stir in the onions and garlic and cook for 5 minutes, or until browned. Add the tomatoes, parsley, salt, and pepper, then bring to a boil and let simmer for 20 minutes, or until the meat is tender.

3 Arrange half the eggplant slices in a layer in an ovenproof dish. Add the meat mixture, then a final layer of the remaining eggplant slices.

4 Beat the eggs in a bowl, then beat in the yogurt and season with salt and pepper. Pour the mixture over the eggplants and sprinkle the grated cheese on top. Bake the moussaka in a preheated oven, 350°F/180°C, for 45 minutes, or until golden brown. Serve straight from the dish.

italian marinated pork chops

ingredients

SERVES 4

4 pork rib chops
4 fresh sage leaves
2 tbsp salted capers
2 gherkins, chopped
small salad, to garnish
garlic bread (optional), to serve

marinade

4 tbsp dry white wine
1 tbsp brown sugar
2 tbsp olive oil
1 tsp Dijon mustard

method

1 Trim any visible fat from the chops and place them in a large, shallow dish. Top each with a sage leaf. Rub the salt off the capers with your fingers and sprinkle them over the chops, together with the gherkins.

2 Mix the wine, sugar, oil, and mustard together in a small bowl and pour the mixture over the chops. Cover with plastic wrap and let marinate in a cool place for about 2 hours.

3 Drain the chops, reserving the marinade. Grill the chops on a hot barbecue for 5 minutes on each side, then grill over medium coals or on a higher rack, turning and brushing occasionally with the reserved marinade, for about 10 minutes more on each side, or until cooked through and tender.

4 Serve at once with a small salad and garlic bread if you like.

herbed pork chops with bleu cheese & walnut butter

ingredients

SERVES 4

4 pork chops
small salad, to serve

marinade

4 tbsp corn oil
2 tbsp lemon juice
1 tbsp chopped fresh marjoram
1 tbsp chopped fresh thyme
2 tbsp chopped fresh parsley
1 garlic clove, finely chopped
1 onion, finely chopped
salt and pepper

bleu cheese & walnut butter

2 oz/55 g butter
4 scallions, finely chopped
5 oz/140 g Gorgonzola or other bleu cheese, crumbled
2 tbsp finely chopped walnuts

method

1 Trim the fat from the chops and place them in a dish. Whisk together the oil, lemon juice, marjoram, thyme, parsley, garlic, and onion in a bowl, then season with salt and pepper. Pour the marinade over the chops, turning to coat. Cover and let marinate in the refrigerator overnight.

2 To make the flavored butter, melt half the butter in a skillet and cook the scallions over low heat, stirring frequently for a few minutes, until softened. Transfer to a bowl and mix in the remaining butter, the cheese, and the walnuts. Form into a roll, then cover and let chill until required.

3 Drain the chops, reserving the marinade. Grill the chops on a hot barbecue for 5 minutes on each side, then grill over medium coals or on a higher rack, turning and brushing occasionally with the reserved marinade, for about 10 minutes more on each side, or until cooked through and tender. Transfer to serving plates and top each chop with 1–2 slices of the cheese and walnut butter. Serve at once with a small salad.

sausages with lentils

ingredients

SERVES 4–6

2 tbsp olive oil
12 merguez sausages
2 onions, chopped finely
2 red bell peppers, cored, seeded, and chopped
1 orange or yellow bell pepper, cored, seeded, and chopped
10 oz/280 g/scant 1½ cups small green lentils, rinsed
1 tsp dried thyme or marjoram
16 fl oz/500 ml/2 cups vegetable stock
salt and pepper
4 tbsp chopped fresh parsley
red wine vinegar, to serve

method

1 Heat the oil in a large, preferably nonstick, lidded skillet over medium-high heat. Add the sausages and cook, stirring frequently, for about 10 minutes until they are brown all over and cooked through; remove from the skillet and set aside.

2 Pour off all but 2 tablespoons of oil from the skillet. Add the onions and bell peppers and cook for about 5 minutes until soft, but not brown. Add the lentils and thyme or marjoram and stir until coated with oil.

3 Stir in the stock and bring to a boil. Reduce the heat, cover, and let simmer for about 30 minutes until the lentils are tender and the liquid is absorbed; if the lentils are tender but too much liquid remains, uncover the skillet and let simmer until it evaporates. Season with salt and pepper.

4 Return the sausages to the skillet and reheat. Stir in the parsley. Serve the sausages with the lentils, then splash a little red wine vinegar over each portion.

greek-style beef kabobs

ingredients

SERVES 4–6

1 small onion, finely chopped
1 tbsp chopped fresh cilantro
large pinch of paprika
1/4 tsp ground allspice
1/4 tsp ground coriander
1/4 tsp brown sugar
1 lb/450 g ground beef
salt and pepper
vegetable oil, for brushing
fresh cilantro leaves, to garnish
freshly cooked bulgur wheat or rice, and mixed salad, to serve

method

1 If you are using wooden skewers, soak them in cold water for 30 minutes before use.

2 Put the onion, fresh cilantro, spices, sugar, and beef into a large bowl and mix until well combined. Season with salt and pepper.

3 On a clean counter, use your hands to shape the mixture into sausages around skewers. Brush them lightly with vegetable oil.

4 Grill the kabobs over hot coals, turning them frequently, for 15–20 minutes, or until cooked right through. Arrange the kabobs on a platter of freshly cooked bulgur wheat or rice and garnish with fresh cilantro leaves. Serve with a mixed salad.

osso bucco with citrus rinds

ingredients

MAKES 12

1–2 tbsp all-purpose flour
salt and pepper
6 meaty slices osso bucco (veal shins)
1–2 tbsp olive oil
9 oz/250 g onions, very finely chopped
9 oz/250 g carrots, finely diced
2 lb 4 oz/1 kg fresh tomatoes, peeled, seeded, and diced, or 1 lb 12 oz/800 g canned chopped tomatoes, drained and passed through a strainer
8 fl oz/250 ml/1 cup dry white wine
8 fl oz/250 ml/1 cup veal stock
6 large basil leaves, torn
1 large garlic clove, very finely chopped
finely grated rind of 1 large lemon
finely grated rind of 1 orange
2 tbsp finely chopped fresh flat-leaf parsley
crusty bread, to serve

method

1 Place the flour in a plastic bag and season with salt and pepper. Add the osso bucco, a couple of pieces at a time, and shake until well coated. Remove and shake off the excess flour. Continue until all the pieces are coated.

2 Heat 1 tablespoon of the oil in a large ovenproof casserole. Add the osso bucco and cook for 10 minutes on each slide until well browned. Remove from the casserole.

3 Add 1–2 teaspoons of oil to the casserole if necessary. Add the onions and cook for 5 minutes, stirring, until softened. Stir in the carrots and continue cooking until they become soft.

4 Add the tomatoes, wine, stock, and basil and return the osso bucco to the casserole. Bring to a boil, then reduce the heat, cover, and let simmer for 1 hour. With the tip of a knife, check that the meat is tender. If not, continue cooking for an additional 10 minutes and test again.

5 When the meat is tender, sprinkle with the garlic, lemon rind, and orange rind, re-cover, and cook for an additional 10 minutes. Adjust the seasoning if necessary. Sprinkle with the parsley and serve with crusty bread.

veal with tuna sauce

ingredients

SERVES 4

1 lb 10 oz/750 g loin of veal, boned
2 carrots, sliced thinly
1 onion, sliced thinly
2 celery stalks, sliced thinly
2 cloves
2 bay leaves
32 fl oz/1 liter/4 cups dry white wine
salt and pepper
lemon slices and chopped fresh flat-leaf parsley, to garnish

tuna sauce

5 oz/140 g canned tuna, drained
4 anchovy fillets, drained and chopped finely
2 oz/55 g/$^1/_2$ cup capers, rinsed and chopped finely
2 oz/55 g/$^1/_2$ cup gherkins, drained and chopped finely
2 egg yolks
4 tbsp lemon juice
4 fl oz/125 ml/$^1/_2$ cup extra-virgin olive oil

method

1 Place the veal in a large, nonmetallic dish and add the carrots, onion, celery, cloves, and bay leaves. Pour in the wine and turn the veal to coat. Cover with plastic wrap and let marinate in the refrigerator overnight.

2 Drain the veal, reserving the marinade. Roll the meat, wrap it in a piece of cheesecloth, and tie it with string. Place in a large pan. Bring the marinade to a boil in another pan. Pour it over the veal with boiling water to cover. Season to taste, bring back to a boil, then reduce the heat, cover, and let simmer for $1^1/_2$ hours, until tender but still firm. Transfer to a plate and set aside to cool, then let chill until ready to serve. Strain the cooking liquid into a bowl and set aside to cool.

3 To make the sauce, put the tuna, anchovies, capers, and gherkins in a food processor and process to make a purée. Beat the egg yolks with the lemon juice in a bowl. Beat in the olive oil, drop by drop to start with and then in a steady stream. Stir in the tuna mixture and about 2 tablespoons of the cooking liquid to give the consistency of heavy cream. Season, cover with plastic wrap, and let chill.

4 To serve, unwrap the veal and pat it dry with paper towels. Cut into $^1/_8$–$^1/_4$-inch thick slices and arrange them on a serving platter. Stir the tuna sauce and spoon it over the veal. Garnish with lemon slices and parsley.

paella with pork & chorizo

ingredients

SERVES 4–6

42 fl oz/1.3 liters/5 1/4 cups fish stock or water
12 large raw shrimp, in their shells
1/2 tsp saffron threads
2 tbsp hot water
3 1/2 oz/100 g skinless, boneless chicken breast, cut into 1/2-inch/1-cm pieces
3 1/2 oz/100 g pork tenderloin, cut into 1/2-inch/1-cm pieces
3 tbsp olive oil
3 1/2 oz/100 g chorizo sausage, casing removed, cut into 1/2-inch/1-cm slices
1 large red onion, chopped
2 garlic cloves, crushed
1/2 tsp cayenne pepper
1/2 tsp paprika
1 red bell pepper and 1 green bell pepper, seeded and sliced
12 cherry tomatoes, halved
13 oz/375 g/generous 1 1/2 cups medium-grain paella rice
1 tbsp chopped fresh parsley
2 tsp chopped fresh tarragon
salt and pepper

method

1 Put the stock in a pan and bring to a simmer. Add the shrimp and cook for 2 minutes, then transfer to a bowl and set aside. Let the stock simmer. Put the saffron threads and water in a bowl and let infuse.

2 Season the chicken and pork to taste. Heat the oil in a paella pan and cook the chicken, pork, and chorizo over medium heat, stirring, for 5 minutes, or until golden. Add the onion and cook, stirring, until softened. Add the garlic, cayenne pepper, paprika, and saffron and its soaking liquid and cook, stirring constantly, for 1 minute. Add the bell peppers and tomato halves and cook, stirring, for 2 minutes.

3 Add the rice and herbs and cook, stirring constantly, for 1 minute to coat. Pour in about 40 fl oz/1.25 liters/5 cups of the stock and bring to a boil, then simmer, uncovered, for 10 minutes. Do not stir during cooking, but shake the pan once or twice, and when adding ingredients. Season to taste and cook for 10 minutes more, or until the rice grains are plump and almost cooked. Add a little more stock if necessary. Add the shrimp and cook for 2 minutes more.

4 When all the liquid has been absorbed and you detect a faint toasty aroma coming from the rice, remove from the heat immediately. Cover with foil and let stand for 5 minutes.

paella primavera

ingredients

SERVES 4–6

1/2 tsp saffron threads
2 tbsp hot water
3 tbsp olive oil
6 oz/175 g serrano ham, diced
1 large carrot, diced
51/2 oz/150 g white mushrooms
4 large scallions, diced
2 garlic cloves, crushed
1 tsp paprika
1/4 tsp cayenne pepper
8 oz/225 g tomatoes, peeled and cut into wedges
1 red bell pepper, halved and seeded, then broiled, peeled, and sliced
1 green bell pepper, halved and seeded, then broiled, peeled, and sliced
12 oz/350 g/15/8 cups medium-grain paella rice
2 tbsp chopped mixed fresh herbs, plus extra to garnish
31/2 fl oz/100 ml/1/3 cup white wine
40 fl oz/1.25 liters/5 cups simmering chicken stock
2 oz/55 g/3/8 cup shelled peas
31/2 oz/100 g fresh asparagus spears, blanched
salt and pepper
lemon wedges, to serve

method

1 Put the saffron threads and water in a small bowl and let infuse for a few minutes.

2 Heat 2 tablespoons of the oil in a paella pan and cook the ham over medium heat, stirring, for 5 minutes. Transfer to a bowl. Heat the remaining oil in the pan and cook the carrot, stirring, for 3 minutes. Add the mushrooms and cook, stirring, for 2 minutes. Add the scallions, garlic, paprika, cayenne pepper, and saffron and its soaking liquid and cook, stirring, for 1 minute. Add the tomatoes and bell peppers and cook, stirring, for 2 minutes.

3 Add the rice and herbs and cook, stirring, for 1 minute, to coat the rice. Pour in the wine and most of the hot stock and bring to a boil, then let simmer, uncovered, for 10 minutes. Do not stir during cooking, but shake the pan once or twice and when adding ingredients. Add the peas and season to taste. Cook for 10 minutes, or until the rice is almost cooked, adding a little more stock if necessary. Return the ham and any juices to the pan. Arrange the asparagus around the paella in a wheel pattern and cook for 2 minutes.

4 When all the liquid has been absorbed and you detect a faint toasty aroma coming from the rice, remove from the heat. Cover with foil and let stand for 5 minutes. Sprinkle over chopped herbs to garnish and serve with lemon wedges.

moroccan chicken

ingredients

SERVES 4

marinade

3 tbsp olive oil
4 tbsp lemon juice
2 tbsp chopped fresh parsley
2 tbsp chopped fresh cilantro
1 garlic clove, finely chopped
1 tsp ground coriander
1/2 tsp ground cumin
1 tsp sweet paprika
pinch of chili powder
4 skinless, boneless chicken breasts, about 5 oz/140 g each

salad

7 oz/200 g raw carrots
7 oz/200 g raw white cabbage
3 1/2 oz/100 g sprouting beans
1 3/4 oz/50 g alfalfa sprouts
1 3/4 oz/50 g golden raisins
1 3/4 oz/50 g raisins
1 tbsp lemon juice
toasted flat breads

method

1 Mix together the oil, lemon juice, parsley, fresh cilantro, garlic, ground coriander, cumin, paprika, and chili powder in a large, shallow, nonmetallic dish.

2 Using a sharp knife, score the chicken breasts 3–4 times. Add the chicken to the dish, turning to coat. Cover with plastic wrap and let marinate in a cool place, turning occasionally, for 2–3 hours.

3 Drain the chicken, reserving the marinade. Grill over hot coals, brushing occasionally with the reserved marinade, for 20–30 minutes, or until tender and cooked through. Season with salt and pepper.

4 Meanwhile, to make the salad, trim and peel the carrots, then grate them into a large salad bowl. Trim the white cabbage, then shred it finely. Transfer it to a large colander and rinse under cold running water. Drain well, then add it to the carrots. Put the sprouting beans and alfalfa sprouts into the colander and rinse well, then drain and add to the salad. Rinse and drain the golden raisins and raisins and add them to the bowl. Pour in the lemon juice and toss the salad into it.

5 Serve the Moroccan chicken with the salad and toasted flat breads.

chicken tagine

ingredients

SERVES 4

1 tbsp olive oil
1 onion, cut into small wedges
2–4 garlic cloves, sliced
1 lb/450 g skinless, boneless chicken breast, diced
1 tsp ground cumin
2 cinnamon sticks, lightly bruised
1 tbsp all-purpose whole wheat flour
8 oz/225 g eggplant, diced
1 red bell pepper, seeded and chopped
3 oz/85 g white mushrooms, sliced
1 tbsp tomato paste
20 fl oz/625 ml/2 1/2 cups chicken stock
10 oz/280 g canned chickpeas, drained and rinsed
2 oz/55 g/1/3 cup no-soak dried apricots, chopped
salt and pepper
1 tbsp chopped fresh cilantro

method

1 Heat the oil in a large pan over medium heat, add the onion and garlic and cook for 3 minutes, stirring frequently. Add the chicken and cook, stirring constantly, for an additional 5 minutes, or until sealed on all sides. Add the cumin and cinnamon sticks to the pan halfway through sealing the chicken.

2 Sprinkle in the flour and cook, stirring constantly, for 2 minutes. Add the eggplant, red bell pepper, and mushrooms and cook for an additional 2 minutes, stirring constantly.

3 Blend the tomato paste with the stock, stir into the pan, and bring to a boil. Reduce the heat and add the chickpeas and apricots. Cover and let simmer for 15–20 minutes, or until the chicken is tender.

4 Season with salt and pepper and serve at once, sprinkled with cilantro.

spanish chicken with preserved lemons

ingredients

SERVES 4

1 tbsp all-purpose flour
4 chicken quarters, skin on
2 tbsp olive oil
2 garlic cloves, crushed
1 large Spanish onion, thinly sliced
24 fl oz/750 ml/3 cups low-salt chicken stock
1/2 tsp saffron threads
2 yellow bell peppers, seeded and cut into chunks
2 preserved lemons, cut into quarters
9 oz/250 g/generous 1 1/4 cups brown basmati rice
white pepper
12 pimiento-stuffed green olives
chopped fresh parsley, to garnish

method

1 Put the flour into a large freezer bag. Add the chicken, close the top of the bag, and shake to coat with flour.

2 Heat the oil in a large skillet over low heat, add the garlic, and cook for 1 minute, stirring constantly. Add the chicken to the skillet and cook over medium heat, turning frequently, for 5 minutes, or until the skin has lightly browned, then remove to a plate. Add the onion to the skillet and cook, stirring occasionally, for 10 minutes until soft.

3 Meanwhile, put the stock and saffron into a pan over low heat and heat through.

4 Transfer the chicken and onion to a large casserole dish, add the yellow bell peppers, lemons, and rice, then pour over the stock. Mix well and season with pepper.

5 Cover and cook in a preheated oven, 350°F/180°C, for 50 minutes, or until the chicken is cooked through and tender. Reduce the oven temperature to 325°F/160°C. Add the olives to the casserole and cook for an additional 10 minutes.

6 Serve sprinkled with chopped parsley.

chicken in tarragon sauce

ingredients

SERVES 4

4 boneless chicken breasts, about 6 oz/175 g each
salt and pepper
1 oz/30 g unsalted butter
1 tbsp sunflower-seed oil

tarragon sauce

2 tbsp tarragon-flavored vinegar
6 tbsp dry white wine
9 fl oz/250 ml/generous 1 cup chicken stock
4 sprigs of fresh tarragon, plus 2 tbsp chopped fresh tarragon
10 fl oz/300 ml/1¼ cups sour cream or heavy cream

method

1 Season the chicken breasts on both sides with salt and pepper. Over medium-high heat, melt the butter with the oil in a skillet large enough to hold the chicken pieces in a single layer. Add the chicken breasts, skin-side down, and sauté until golden brown.

2 Transfer the chicken breasts to a roasting pan and roast in a preheated oven, 375°F/190°C, for 15–20 minutes, or until they are tender and the juices run clear when a skewer is inserted into the thickest part of the meat. Transfer the chicken to a serving platter and cover with foil, shiny-side down, then set aside.

3 To make the tarragon sauce, skim the excess fat from the cooking juices. Place the roasting pan over medium-high heat and add the vinegar, scraping any sediment from the bottom of the tin. Pour in the wine and bring to a boil, still stirring and scraping, and boil until the liquid is reduced by half.

4 Stir in the stock and whole tarragon sprigs and continue boiling until the liquid reduces to about 4 fl oz/125 ml/½ cup. Stir in the sour cream and continue boiling to reduce the sauce by half. Discard the tarragon sprigs, and adjust the seasoning if necessary. Stir the chopped tarragon into the sauce.

5 To serve, slice the chicken breasts on individual plates and spoon over the sauce.

filo chicken pie

ingredients

SERVES 6–8

- 3 lb 5 oz/1.5 kg whole chicken
- 1 small onion, halved, and 3 large onions, chopped finely
- 1 carrot, sliced thickly
- 1 celery stalk, sliced thickly
- pared rind of 1 lemon
- 1 bay leaf
- 10 peppercorns
- 5½ oz/155 g butter
- 2 oz/55 g/scant ½ cup all-purpose flour
- 5 fl oz/150 ml/⅔ cup milk
- salt and pepper
- 1 oz/25 g/⅓ cup kefalotiri or romano cheese, grated
- 3 eggs, beaten
- 8 oz/225 g filo pastry (work with one sheet at a time and keep the remaining sheets covered with a damp dish towel)

method

1 Put the chicken in a large pan with the halved onion, carrot, celery, lemon rind, bay leaf, and peppercorns. Add cold water to cover and bring to a boil. Cover and simmer for about 1 hour, or until the chicken is cooked.

2 Remove the chicken and set aside to cool. Bring the stock to a boil and boil until reduced to about 20 fl oz/625 ml/2½ cups. Strain and reserve the stock. Cut the cooled chicken into bite-size pieces, discarding the skin and bones.

3 Fry the chopped onions until softened in 2 oz/55 g of the butter. Add the flour and cook gently, stirring, for 1–2 minutes. Gradually stir in the reserved stock and the milk. Bring to a boil, stirring constantly, then simmer for 1–2 minutes until thick and smooth. Remove from the heat, add the chicken, and season. Let cool, then stir in the cheese and eggs.

4 Melt the remaining butter and use a little to grease a deep 12 x 8-inch/30 x 20-cm metal baking pan. Cut the pastry sheets in half widthwise. Line the pan with one sheet of pastry and brush it with a little melted butter. Repeat with half of the pastry sheets. Spread the filling over the pastry, then top with the remaining pastry sheets, brushing each with butter and tucking down the edges.

5 Score the top of the pie into 6 or 8 squares. Bake in a preheated oven, 375°F/190°C, for about 50 minutes, until golden. Serve warm.

chicken kabobs with yogurt sauce

ingredients

SERVES 4

10 fl oz/300 ml/1¼ cups strained plain yogurt
2 garlic cloves, crushed
juice of ½ lemon
1 tbsp chopped fresh herbs such as oregano, dill, tarragon, or parsley
salt and pepper
4 large skinned, boned chicken breasts
corn oil, for oiling
8 firm stems of fresh rosemary, optional
shredded romaine lettuce and rice, to serve
lemon wedges, to garnish

method

1 To make the sauce, put the yogurt, garlic, lemon juice, herbs, salt, and pepper in a large bowl and mix well together.

2 Cut the chicken breasts into chunks measuring about 1½ inches/4 cm square. Add to the yogurt mixture and toss well together until the chicken pieces are coated. Cover and leave to marinate in the refrigerator for about 1 hour. If you are using wooden skewers, soak them in cold water for 30 minutes before use.

3 Preheat the broiler. Thread the pieces of chicken onto 8 flat, oiled metal kabob skewers, wooden skewers, or rosemary stems and place on an oiled broiler pan.

4 Cook the kabobs under the broiler for about 15 minutes, turning and basting with the remaining marinade occasionally, until lightly browned and tender.

5 Pour the remaining marinade into a pan and heat gently but do not boil. Serve the kabobs with shredded lettuce on a bed of rice, and garnish with lemon wedges. Accompany with the yogurt sauce.

pesto & ricotta chicken with tomato vinaigrette

ingredients

SERVES 4

1 tbsp pesto sauce
115 g/4 oz/1/2 cup ricotta cheese
4 x 175 g/6 oz boneless chicken breasts
1 tbsp olive oil
pepper
small salad, to garnish

tomato vinaigrette

3 1/2 fl oz/100 ml/scant 1/2 cup olive oil
1 bunch fresh chives
500 g/1 lb 2 oz tomatoes, peeled, seeded, and chopped
juice and finely grated rind of 1 lime
salt and pepper

method

1 Mix together the pesto and ricotta in a small bowl until well combined. Using a sharp knife, cut a deep slit in the side of each chicken breast to make a pocket. Spoon the ricotta mixture into the pockets and re-shape the chicken breasts to enclose it. Place the chicken on a plate, cover, and let chill for 30 minutes.

2 To make the vinaigrette, pour the olive oil into a blender or food processor, add the chives, and process until smooth. Scrape the mixture into a bowl and stir in the tomatoes, lime juice, and rind. Season with salt and pepper.

3 Brush the chicken with the olive oil and season with pepper. Grill on a fairly hot barbecue for about 8 minutes on each side, or until cooked through and tender. Transfer to serving plates, spoon over the vinaigrette, and serve immediately.

fish & seafood

Mediterranean countries enjoy the benefits of countless miles of coastline, and fish, a high-protein, low-fat food rich in vitamin B12, iron, and the essential omega 3 fatty acids, is one of the key ingredients of the health-enhancing Mediterranean diet.

Fish and seafood are caught and landed every day and cooked fresh from the sea. The simplest method is to roast, broil, grill, or pan-fry the fish with olive oil, lemon, and herbs but, with such wonderful bounty at their disposal, the inhabitants of the various Mediterranean countries have become marvelously creative with their fish dishes!

Fish stews are an obvious way to use the daily catch, because a variety of fish and seafood can go into them, depending on what has been landed in the nearest harbor. Try Marseilles-style Fish Stew, a specialty of the famous French coastal town, Livornese Seafood Stew from the Tuscan port of Livorna in Italy, Spanish Swordfish Stew, or Moroccan Fish Tagine.

If you prefer to keep it simple, there are some great options, such as Cod with Catalan Spinach, Broiled Red Snapper with Garlic, Chargrilled Sea Bass with Stewed Artichokes, and Sicilian Tuna. They are uncomplicated and so good—try them all!

roasted monkfish

ingredients

SERVES 4

1 lb 8 oz/675 g monkfish tail, skinned

4–5 large garlic cloves, peeled

salt and pepper

3 tbsp olive oil

1 onion, cut into wedges

1 small eggplant, about $10^1/_2$ oz/300 g, cut into chunks

1 red bell pepper, seeded, cut into wedges

1 yellow bell pepper, seeded, cut into wedges

1 large zucchini, about 8 oz/225 g, cut into wedges

1 tbsp shredded fresh basil

method

1 Remove the central bone from the fish, if not already removed, and make small slits down each fillet. Cut 2 of the garlic cloves into thin slivers and insert into the fish. Place the fish on a sheet of waxed paper, season with salt and pepper, and drizzle over 1 tablespoon of the oil. Bring the top edges together. Form into a pleat and fold over, then fold the ends underneath, completely encasing the fish. Set aside.

2 Put the remaining garlic cloves and all the vegetables into a roasting pan and sprinkle with the remaining oil, turning the vegetables so that they are well coated in the oil.

3 Roast in a preheated oven, 400°F/200°C, for 20 minutes, turning occasionally. Put the fish package on top of the vegetables and cook for an additional 15–20 minutes, or until the vegetables are tender and the fish is cooked.

4 Remove from the oven and open up the package. Cut the monkfish into thick slices. Arrange the vegetables on warmed serving plates, top with the fish slices, and sprinkle with the basil. Serve at once.

basque-style cod

ingredients

SERVES 4

3 tbsp olive oil
4 cod fillets, about 6 oz/175 g each, all skin and bones removed, rinsed and patted dry
1 tbsp all-purpose flour
salt and pepper
1 large onion, finely chopped
4 large tomatoes, peeled, seeded, and chopped
2 large garlic cloves, crushed
5 fl oz/150 ml/2/3 cup dry white wine
1/2 tsp paprika, to taste
2 red bell peppers, chargrilled, peeled and seeded, then cut into strips
2 green bell peppers, chargrilled, peeled and seeded, then cut into strips
zest of 1 lemon, in broad strips
finely chopped fresh flat-leaf parsley, to garnish

method

1 Heat 1 tablespoon of the oil in a flameproof casserole over medium-high heat. Very lightly dust one side of each cod fillet with the flour, seasoned with salt and pepper.

2 Pan-fry, floured-side down, for 2 minutes, or until just golden. Set aside. Wipe out the casserole, then heat the remaining oil over medium-high heat. Add the onion and sauté for 5 minutes, or until soft but not browned.

3 Stir in the tomatoes, garlic, wine, paprika, salt, and pepper and bring to a boil. Reduce the heat and simmer for 5 minutes, stirring occasionally.

4 Stir the red and green bell peppers into the casserole, with the lemon strips, and bring to a boil. Lay the cod fillets on top, browned-side up, and season with salt and pepper. Cover the casserole and bake in a preheated oven, 400°F/200°C, for 12–15 minutes, depending on the thickness of the cod, until it is cooked through and flakes easily.

5 Discard the lemon zest just before serving. Serve the cod on a bed of the vegetables and sprinkled with the chopped parsley.

cod with catalan spinach

ingredients

SERVES 4

catalan spinach

- 2 oz/55g/1/2 cup raisins
- 2 oz/55g/1/2 cup pine nuts
- 4 tbsp extra-virgin olive oil
- 3 garlic cloves, crushed
- 1 lb 2oz/500 g baby spinach leaves, rinsed and shaken dry
- 4 cod fillets, each about 6 oz/175 g
- olive oil
- salt and pepper
- tomato halves and lemon wedges, to serve

method

1 Put the raisins for the Catalan spinach in a small bowl, cover with hot water, and set aside to soak for 15 minutes. Drain well.

2 Meanwhile, put the pine nuts in a dry skillet over medium-high heat and dry-fry for 1–2 minutes, shaking frequently, until toasted and golden brown: watch closely because they burn quickly.

3 Heat the oil in a large, lidded skillet over medium-high heat. Add the garlic and cook for 2 minutes, or until golden, but not brown. Remove with a slotted spoon and discard.

4 Add the spinach to the oil, with only the rinsing water clinging to its leaves. Cover and cook for 4–5 minutes until wilted. Uncover, stir in the drained raisins and pine nuts and continue cooking until all the liquid evaporates. Season and keep warm.

5 To cook the cod, brush the fillets lightly with oil and sprinkle with salt and pepper. Place under a preheated hot broiler about 4 inches/10 cm from the heat and broil for 8–10 minutes until the flesh is opaque and flakes easily.

6 Divide the spinach among 4 plates and place the cod fillets on top. Serve with the tomato halves and lemon wedges.

skate in mustard & caper sauce

ingredients

SERVES 4

2 skate wings

mustard & caper sauce

2 tbsp olive oil
1 onion, chopped finely
1 garlic clove, chopped finely
5 fl oz/150 ml/$^{2}/_{3}$ cup strained plain yogurt
1 tsp lemon juice
1 tbsp chopped fresh flat-leaf parsley, plus extra to garnish
1 tbsp capers, chopped coarsely
1 tbsp wholegrain mustard
salt and pepper
lemon wedges, to serve

method

1 Cut each skate wing in half and place in a large skillet. Cover with salted water, bring to a boil, then simmer for 10–15 minutes, until tender.

2 Meanwhile, make the mustard and caper sauce. Heat the oil in a pan, add the onion and garlic, and cook for 5 minutes, until softened. Add the yogurt, lemon juice, parsley, and capers and cook for 1–2 minutes, until heated through. (Do not boil, or the sauce will curdle.) Stir in the mustard and season with salt and pepper.

3 Drain the skate and put on four warmed serving plates. Pour over the sauce and sprinkle with chopped parsley.

4 Serve hot, with lemon wedges.

marseilles-style fish stew

ingredients

SERVES 4–6

large pinch of saffron threads
2 tbsp olive oil
1 large onion, finely chopped
1 bulb of fennel, thinly sliced, with the feathery green fronds reserved
2 large garlic cloves, crushed
4 tbsp pastis
32 fl oz/1 liter/4 cups fish stock
2 large sun-ripened tomatoes, peeled, seeded and diced, or 14 oz/400 g chopped tomatoes, drained
1 tbsp tomato paste
1 bay leaf
pinch of sugar
pinch of dried chile flakes (optional)
salt and pepper
24 large raw shrimp, shelled
1 squid, cleaned and cut into 1/4-inch/5-mm rings, tentacles reserved
2 lb/900 g fresh, skinned and boned Mediterranean fish, such as sea bass, monkfish, red snapper, halibut, or haddock, cut into large chunks

method

1 Put the saffron threads in a small dry skillet over high heat and toast, stirring constantly, for 1 minute, or until you can smell the aroma. Immediately tip out of the pan and set aside.

2 Heat the oil in a large flameproof casserole over medium heat. Add the onion and fennel and sauté for 3 minutes, then add the garlic and sautée for an additional 5 minutes, until the onion and fennel are soft, but not colored.

3 Remove the casserole from the heat. Warm the pastis in a ladle or small pan, then ignite and pour it over the onion and fennel to flambé. When the flames die down, return the casserole to the heat and stir in the stock, tomatoes, tomato paste, bay leaf, sugar, chile flakes, if using, salt, and pepper. Slowly bring to a boil, skimming the surface if necessary, then reduce the heat to low and simmer, uncovered, for 15 minutes.

4 Add the prepared shrimp and squid rings and simmer until the shrimp turn pink and the squid rings are opaque. Do not overcook, or they will be tough. Use a slotted spoon to transfer to serving bowls. Add the fish chunks to the broth and simmer just until the flesh flakes easily. Remove smaller, thinner pieces first. Transfer the seafood and broth to the serving bowls and garnish with the reserved fennel fronds.

livornese seafood stew

ingredients

SERVES 8

12 oz/350 g freshly cooked lobster meat
12 oz/350 g prepared squid, sliced into rings
3 lb/1.3 kg red snapper or gurnard fillets, sliced thickly
2 lb/900 g cod fillet, sliced thickly
2 lb/900 g tilapia or monkfish fillets, sliced thickly
salt and pepper
5 fl oz/150 ml/2/3 cup virgin olive oil
2 onions, chopped
1 carrot, chopped
2 celery stalks, chopped
12 fl oz/350 ml/1 1/2 cups dry white wine
72 fl oz/2.25 liters/9 cups water
14 oz/400 g canned tomatoes
1 bay leaf
1 fresh red chile, seeded
1 ciabatta or baguette, cut into 1/2-inch slices
4 garlic cloves, sliced thinly
2 lb/900 g live mussels, scrubbed and debearded*
4 fresh sage leaves

* discard any mussels that remain closed after cooking

method

1 Season the lobster meat, squid, and fish fillets with salt and pepper and set aside.

2 Heat 4 tablespoons of the oil in a pan. Cook the onions, carrot, and celery over medium heat, stirring, until just starting to color. Add 10 fl oz/300 ml/1 1/4 cups of the wine, the water, tomatoes, bay leaf, and chile. Bring to a boil, then let simmer for 50 minutes. Strain the stock and set aside 40 fl oz/1.25 liters/5 cups.

3 Place the bread slices on a cookie sheet and drizzle with 2 tablespoons of the olive oil. Bake in a preheated oven, 400°F/200°C, for about 10 minutes, until crisp, then rub each slice with one of the garlic cloves and set aside.

4 Put the mussels in a pan, add the remaining wine, cover, and cook over high heat, shaking the pan occasionally, until the shells have opened. Strain, reserving the cooking liquid.

5 Finely chop the remaining garlic. Heat the remaining olive oil in a pan, add the sage and chopped garlic, and cook for 1 minute. Add the squid and cook, stirring, for 2–3 minutes, until golden. Remove with a slotted spoon.

6 Add the fish fillets and stock to the pan and bring to a boil, then let simmer for 5 minutes. Return the squid to the pan and add the mussels, lobster meat, and 2 tablespoons of the reserved cooking liquid. Heat through for 2 minutes. Serve at once with the garlic toasts.

spanish swordfish stew

ingredients

SERVES 4

4 tbsp olive oil
3 shallots, chopped
2 garlic cloves, chopped
8 oz/225 g canned chopped tomatoes
1 tbsp tomato paste
1 lb 7 oz/650 g potatoes, sliced
9 fl oz/250 ml/generous 1 cup vegetable stock
2 tbsp lemon juice
1 red bell pepper, seeded and chopped
1 orange bell pepper, seeded and chopped
20 black olives, pitted and halved
2 lb 4 oz/1 kg swordfish steak, skinned and cut into bite-size pieces
salt and pepper
fresh flat-leaf parsley sprigs and lemon slices, to garnish

method

1 Heat the oil in a pan over low heat, add the shallots, and cook, stirring frequently, for 4 minutes, or until softened. Add the garlic, tomatoes, and tomato paste, cover, and let simmer gently for 20 minutes.

2 Meanwhile, put the potatoes in an ovenproof casserole with the stock and lemon juice. Bring to a boil, then reduce the heat and add the bell peppers. Cover and cook for 15 minutes.

3 Add the olives, swordfish, and the tomato mixture to the potatoes. Season with salt and pepper. Stir well, then cover and let simmer for 7–10 minutes, or until the swordfish is cooked to your taste.

4 Remove from the heat and garnish with parsley sprigs and lemon slices.

chargrilled sea bass with stewed artichokes

ingredients

SERVES 6

- 4 lb/1.8 kg baby globe artichokes
- $2^{1}/_{2}$ tbsp fresh lemon juice, plus the cut halves of the lemon
- 5 fl oz/150 ml/$^{2}/_{3}$ cup olive oil
- 10 garlic cloves, finely sliced
- 1 tbsp chopped fresh thyme, plus extra to garnish
- salt and pepper
- 6 x 4-oz/115-g sea bass fillets
- 1 tbsp olive oil, for brushing
- crusty bread, to serve

method

1 Peel away the tough outer leaves of each artichoke until the yellow-green heart is revealed. Slice off the pointed top at about halfway between the point and the top of the stem. Cut off the stem and pare off what is left of the dark green leaves around the bottom of the artichoke.

2 Submerge the prepared artichokes in water containing the cut halves of the lemon, to prevent discoloration. When all the artichokes have been prepared, turn them choke side down and slice thickly.

3 Heat the olive oil in a large pan. Add the artichoke pieces, garlic, thyme, lemon juice, and seasoning, cover, and cook over low heat for 20–30 minutes, without coloring, until tender.

4 Meanwhile, preheat a ridged stovetop grill pan or light a barbecue. Brush the sea bass fillets with the 1 tablespoon olive oil and season well. Cook on the grill pan or over hot coals for 3–4 minutes on each side until just tender.

5 Divide the stewed artichokes among 6 plates and top each with a fish fillet. Garnish with chopped thyme and serve with crusty bread.

porgy wrapped in grape leaves

ingredients

SERVES 4

2 porgy, about 12 oz/350 g each, cleaned and scaled
thyme leaves and half a grilled lemon, to garnish
12–16 large grape leaves

marinade

6 tbsp olive oil
2 tbsp white wine or dry sherry
2 garlic cloves, finely chopped
2 bay leaves, crumbled
1 tbsp fresh thyme leaves
1 tbsp snipped fresh chives
salt and pepper

method

1 Rinse the fish and pat dry with paper towels. Score each fish 2–3 times diagonally on each side and place in a large dish. Mix together the olive oil, white wine, garlic, bay leaves, thyme, and chives in a small bowl and season with salt and pepper. Spoon the mixture over the fish, turning to coat. Cover and let marinate for 1 hour.

2 If using grape leaves preserved in brine, soak them in hot water for 20 minutes, then rinse well and pat dry. If using fresh grape leaves, blanch in boiling water for 3 minutes, then refresh under cold water, drain, and pat dry.

3 Drain the fish, reserving the marinade. Wrap each fish in grape leaves to enclose. Brush with the marinade. Grill on a medium barbecue for 6 minutes on each side, brushing with more marinade occasionally.

4 Serve garnished with thyme leaves and half a grilled lemon.

broiled red snapper with garlic

ingredients

SERVES 4

- 2 tbsp lemon juice
- 4 tbsp olive oil, plus extra for oiling
- salt and pepper
- 4 red snapper or mullet, scaled and gutted
- 2 tbsp chopped fresh herbs such as oregano, marjoram, flat-leaf parsley, or thyme
- 2 garlic cloves, chopped finely
- 2 tbsp chopped fresh flat-leaf parsley
- lemon wedges, to garnish

method

1 Preheat the broiler. Put the lemon juice, oil, salt, and pepper in a bowl and whisk together. Brush the mixture inside and on both sides of the fish and sprinkle on the chopped herb of your choice. Place on an oiled broiler pan.

2 Broil the fish for about 10 minutes, basting frequently and turning once, until golden brown.

3 Meanwhile, mix together the chopped garlic and chopped parsley. Sprinkle the garlic mixture on top of the cooked fish and serve hot or cold, garnished with lemon wedges.

moroccan fish tagine

ingredients

SERVES 4

2 tbsp olive oil
1 large onion, finely chopped
large pinch of saffron threads
1/2 tsp ground cinnamon
1 tsp ground coriander
1/2 tsp ground cumin
1/2 tsp ground turmeric
7 oz/200 g canned chopped tomatoes
10 fl oz/300 ml/1 1/4 cups fish stock
4 small red snapper, cleaned, boned, and heads and tails removed
1 3/4 oz/50 g/1/3 cup pitted green olives
1 tbsp chopped preserved lemon
3 tbsp chopped fresh cilantro
salt and pepper
freshly prepared couscous or crusty bread, to serve

method

1 Heat the oil in a large pan or ovenproof casserole over low heat, add the onion, and cook, stirring occasionally, for 10 minutes until softened, but not browned. Add the saffron, cinnamon, coriander, cumin, and turmeric and cook, stirring constantly, for an additional 30 seconds.

2 Add the tomatoes and stock and stir well. Bring to a boil, then reduce the heat, cover, and let simmer for 15 minutes. Uncover and let simmer for an additional 20–35 minutes until thickened.

3 Cut each snapper in half, then add the pieces to the pan, pushing them into the sauce. Let simmer gently for an additional 5–6 minutes until the fish is just cooked.

4 Carefully stir in the olives, preserved lemon, and cilantro. Season with salt and pepper and serve with couscous, or crusty bread.

red snapper with capers & olives

ingredients

SERVES 4

1 lb 9 oz/700 g red snapper fillets (about 12)
3 tbsp chopped fresh marjoram or flat-leaf parsley
salt and pepper
thinly peeled rind of 1 orange, cut into thin strips
8 oz/225 g mixed salad greens, torn into pieces
6 fl oz/175 ml/3/4 cup extra-virgin olive oil
1 tbsp balsamic vinegar
1 tbsp white wine vinegar
1 tsp Dijon mustard
3 tbsp virgin olive oil
1 fennel bulb, cut into thin sticks

sauce

1 tbsp butter
1 1/2 oz/40 g/1/4 cup black olives, pitted and sliced thinly
1 tbsp capers, rinsed

method

1 Place the fish fillets on a large plate, sprinkle with the marjoram, and season with salt and pepper. Set aside.

2 Blanch the orange rind in a small pan of boiling water for 2 minutes, drain, refresh under cold water, and drain well again.

3 Place the mixed salad greens in a large bowl. Whisk together the extra-virgin olive oil, balsamic vinegar, wine vinegar, and mustard in a small bowl and season. Pour the dressing over the salad greens and toss well. Arrange on a large serving platter.

4 Heat the virgin olive oil in a heavy-bottom skillet. Add the fennel and cook, stirring constantly, for 1 minute. Remove the fennel with a slotted spoon, set aside, and keep warm. Add the fish fillets, skin-side down, and cook for 2 minutes. Carefully turn them over and cook for an additional 1–2 minutes. Remove from the skillet and drain on paper towels. Keep warm.

5 To make the sauce, melt the butter in a small pan, add the olives and capers, and cook, stirring constantly, for 1 minute.

6 Place the fish fillets on the bed of salad greens, top with the orange rind and fennel, and pour over the sauce. Serve at once.

sicilian tuna

ingredients

SERVES 4

marinade

- 4 fl oz/125 ml/1/2 cup extra-virgin olive oil
- 4 garlic cloves, chopped finely
- 4 fresh red chiles, seeded and chopped finely
- juice and finely grated rind of 2 lemons
- 4 tbsp finely chopped fresh flat-leaf parsley
- salt and pepper

- 4 x 5-oz/140-g tuna steaks
- 2 fennel bulbs, sliced thickly lengthwise
- 2 red onions, sliced
- 2 tbsp virgin olive oil
- rocket salad and crusty bread, to serve

method

1 First, make the marinade by whisking all the ingredients together in a bowl. Place the tuna steaks in a large shallow dish and spoon over 4 tablespoons of the marinade, turning to coat. Cover and set aside for 30 minutes. Set aside the remaining marinade.

2 Heat a cast-iron ridged grill pan. Put the fennel and onions in a bowl, add the oil, and toss well to coat. Add to the grill pan and cook for 5 minutes on each side, until just starting to color. Transfer to 4 warmed serving plates, drizzle with the reserved marinade, and keep warm.

3 Add the tuna steaks to the grill pan and cook, turning once, for 4–5 minutes, until firm to the touch but still moist inside. Transfer the tuna to the plates and serve immediately with the rocket salad and crusty bread.

salad niçoise

ingredients

SERVES 4–6
AS AN ENTRÉE

- 2 tuna steaks, about 3/4 inch/2 cm thick
- olive oil
- salt and pepper
- 9 oz/250 g green beans, trimmed
- garlic vinaigrette
- 2 hearts of lettuce, leaves separated
- 3 large hard-cooked eggs, cut into fourths
- 2 juicy vine-ripened tomatoes, cut into wedges
- 1 3/4 oz/50 g anchovy fillets in oil, drained
- 2 oz/55 g black olives
- torn fresh basil leaves, to garnish

method

1 Heat a ridged cast-iron grill pan over high heat until you can feel the heat rising from the surface. Brush the tuna steaks with oil, then place, oiled-side down, on the hot pan and chargrill for 2 minutes.

2 Lightly brush the top side of the tuna steaks with a little more oil. Use a pair of tongs to turn the tuna steaks over, then season with salt and pepper. Continue chargilling for an additional 2 minutes for rare or up to 4 minutes for well done. Let cool.

3 Meanwhile, bring a pan of salted water to a boil. Add the beans to the pan and return to a boil, then boil for 3 minutes, or until tender-crisp. Drain the beans and immediately transfer them to a large bowl. Pour over the garlic vinaigrette and stir together, then let the beans cool in the dressing.

4 To serve, line a platter with lettuce leaves. Lift the beans out of the bowl, leaving the excess dressing behind, and pile them in the center of the platter. Break the tuna into large flakes and arrange it over the beans.

5 Arrange the hard-cooked eggs and tomatoes around the side. Place the anchovy fillets over the salad, then scatter with the olives and basil. Drizzle the dressing remaining in the bowl over everything and serve.

broiled tuna & vegetable kabobs

ingredients

SERVES 4

4 tuna steaks, about 5 oz/ 140 g each
2 red onions
12 cherry tomatoes
1 red bell pepper, seeded and diced into 1-inch/2.5-cm pieces
1 yellow bell pepper, seeded and diced into 1-inch/ 2.5-cm pieces
1 zucchini, sliced
1 tbsp chopped fresh oregano
4 tbsp olive oil
pepper
lime wedges, to garnish

method

1 Preheat the broiler to high. Cut the tuna into 1-inch/2.5-cm dice. Peel the onions, leaving the root intact, and cut each onion lengthwise into 6 wedges.

2 Divide the fish and vegetables evenly among 8 wooden skewers (presoaked to avoid burning) and arrange on the broiler pan.

3 Mix the oregano and oil together in a small bowl. Season with pepper. Lightly brush the kabobs with the oil and cook under a broiler preheated to high for 10–15 minutes or until evenly cooked, turning occasionally. If you cannot fit all the kabobs on the broiler pan at once, cook them in batches, keeping the cooked kabobs warm while cooking the remainder. Alternatively, these kabobs can be cooked on a barbecue.

4 Garnish with lime wedges.

fresh sardines baked with lemon & oregano

ingredients

SERVES 4

- 2 lemons, plus extra lemon wedges, to garnish
- 12 large fresh sardines, cleaned
- 4 tbsp olive oil
- 4 tbsp chopped fresh oregano
- salt and pepper

method

1 Slice one of the lemons and grate the rind and squeeze the juice from the second lemon.

2 Cut the heads off the sardines. Put the fish in a shallow, ovenproof dish large enough to hold them in a single layer. Put the lemon slices between the fish. Drizzle the lemon juice and oil over the fish. Sprinkle over the lemon rind and oregano and season with salt and pepper.

3 Bake in a preheated oven, 375°F/190°C, for 20–30 minutes until the fish are tender. Serve garnished with lemon wedges.

north african sardines

ingredients

SERVES 4

1 lb 2 oz/500 g fresh sardines, cleaned and scaled

grilled lemon halves, to garnish

marinade

6 tbsp olive oil

3 tbsp lemon juice

3 tbsp chopped fresh cilantro

2 tsp finely grated lemon rind

1/2 tsp ground cumin

1/4 tsp paprika

salt and pepper

method

1 Place the sardines in a large, shallow dish. Mix together the olive oil, lemon juice, cilantro, lemon rind, cumin, and paprika in a bowl and season with salt and pepper. Pour the mixture over the fish, turning to coat. Cover and let stand in a cool place to marinate for 1 hour.

2 Drain the fish, reserving the marinade. Place the sardines in a wire barbecue basket.

3 Grill on a medium barbecue, brushing frequently with the marinade, for about 3 minutes on each side, or until browned. Serve at once, garnished with grilled lemon halves.

lemon-marinated shrimp with mint pesto

ingredients

SERVES 4

1 lb 10 oz/750 g raw jumbo shrimp
juice of 2 lemons
1 bunch fresh mint, chopped
2 garlic cloves, very finely chopped

mint pesto

1 garlic clove, coarsely chopped
8 tbsp fresh mint, coarsely chopped
3 tbsp extra virgin olive oil
1 tbsp red wine vinegar
1 tbsp sour cream or heavy cream
1 tbsp grated Parmesan cheese
salt and pepper

method

1 Shell and devein the shrimp. Place them in a shallow dish and sprinkle with the lemon juice, mint, and garlic. Toss well to coat, cover, and let marinate for 30 minutes.

2 To make the pesto, put all the ingredients in a blender or food processor and process until smooth. Scrape into a bowl, then cover and let chill until required.

3 Drain the shrimp and thread them onto skewers (presoaked if using wooden ones). Grill on a medium barbecue for 2–3 minutes on each side, or until they have turned pink and are cooked through.

4 Remove the shrimp from the skewers and transfer to serving plates. Add a spoonful of mint pesto and serve.

shrimp pilaf

ingredients

SERVES 4

3 tbsp olive oil

1 onion, chopped finely

1 red bell pepper, cored, seeded and sliced thinly

1 garlic clove, crushed

8 oz/225 g/1 1/3 cups long-grain white rice

24 fl oz/750 ml/3 cups fish, chicken, or vegetable stock

1 bay leaf

salt and pepper

14 oz/400 g shelled, cooked shrimp, thawed and drained if frozen

whole cooked shrimp, lemon wedges, and black Greek olives, to garnish

grated kefalotiri or romano cheese and cubes of feta cheese, to serve

method

1 Heat the oil in a large, lidded skillet, add the onion, red bell pepper, and garlic, and fry for 5 minutes, until softened. Add the rice and cook for 2–3 minutes, stirring all the time, until the grains look transparent.

2 Add the stock, bay leaf, salt, and pepper. Bring to a boil, cover the skillet with a tightly fitting lid, and simmer for about 15 minutes, until the rice is tender and the liquid has been absorbed. Do not stir during cooking. When cooked, very gently stir in the shrimp.

3 Remove the lid, cover the skillet with a clean dish towel, replace the lid, and let stand in a warm place for 10 minutes to dry out. Stir with a fork to separate the grains.

4 Serve garnished with whole shrimp, lemon wedges, and black olives. Accompany with kefalotiri or romano cheese, for sprinkling on top, and a bowl of feta cubes.

seafood paella with lemon & herbs

ingredients

SERVES 4–6

- 1/2 tsp saffron threads
- 2 tbsp hot water
- 5 1/2 oz/150 g cod fillet, skinned and rinsed under cold running water
- 42 fl oz/1.3 liters/5 1/4 cups simmering fish stock
- 12 large raw shrimp, shelled and deveined
- 1 lb/450 g raw squid, cleaned and cut into rings or bite-size pieces (or use the same quantity of shucked scallops)
- 3 tbsp olive oil
- 1 large red onion, chopped
- 2 garlic cloves, crushed
- 1 small fresh red chile, seeded and minced
- 8 oz/225 g tomatoes, peeled and cut into wedges
- 13 oz/375 g/generous 1 1/2 cups medium-grain paella rice
- 1 tbsp chopped fresh parsley
- 2 tsp chopped fresh dill
- salt and pepper
- 1 lemon, cut into halves, to serve

method

1 Put the saffron threads and water in a small bowl and let infuse for a few minutes.

2 Add the cod to the pan of simmering stock and cook for 5 minutes, then transfer to a colander, rinse under cold running water and drain. Add the shrimp and squid to the stock and cook for 2 minutes. Cut the cod into chunks, then transfer, with the other seafood, to a bowl and set aside. Let the stock simmer.

3 Heat the oil in a paella pan and stir the onion over medium heat until softened. Add the garlic, chile, and saffron and its soaking liquid and cook, stirring, for 1 minute. Add the tomato wedges and cook, stirring, for 2 minutes. Add the rice and herbs and cook, stirring, for 1 minute. Add most of the stock and bring to a boil. Let simmer, uncovered, for 10 minutes. Do not stir during cooking, but shake the pan once or twice, and when adding ingredients. Season and cook for 10 minutes, until the rice is almost cooked. Add more stock if necessary. Add the seafood and cook for 2 minutes.

4 When all the liquid has been absorbed and you detect a faint toasty aroma coming from the rice, remove from the heat immediately. Cover with foil and let stand for 5 minutes. Serve with the lemon halves.

paella with mussels & white wine

ingredients

SERVES 4–6

- $5^1/_2$ oz/150 g cod fillet, skinned and rinsed in cold water
- 42 fl oz/1.3 liters/$5^1/_4$ cups simmering fish stock
- 7 oz/200 g live mussels, scrubbed and debearded
- 3 tbsp olive oil
- 1 large red onion, chopped
- 2 garlic cloves, crushed
- $^1/_2$ tsp cayenne pepper
- $^1/_2$ tsp saffron threads infused in 2 tbsp hot water
- 8 oz/225 g tomatoes, peeled and cut into wedges
- 1 red bell pepper, seeded and sliced
- 1 green bell pepper, seeded and sliced
- 13 oz/375 g/generous $1^1/_2$ cups medium-grain paella rice
- $3^1/_2$ fl oz/100 ml/generous $^1/_3$ cup white wine
- $5^1/_2$ oz/150 g/generous 1 cup shelled peas
- 1 tbsp chopped fresh dill, plus extra to garnish
- salt and pepper
- lemon wedges, to serve

method

1 Cook the cod in the pan of simmering stock for 5 minutes. Transfer to a colander, rinse under cold running water, and drain. Cut into chunks, then transfer to a bowl and set aside. Cook the mussels in the stock for 5 minutes, or until opened, then transfer to the bowl with the cod, discarding any that remain closed.

2 Heat the oil in a paella pan and stir the onion over medium heat until softened. Add the garlic, cayenne pepper, and saffron and its soaking liquid and cook, stirring constantly, for 1 minute. Add the tomatoes and bell peppers and cook, stirring, for 2 minutes.

3 Add the rice and cook, stirring, for 1 minute. Add the wine and most of the stock and bring to a boil, then let simmer for 10 minutes. Do not stir during cooking, but shake the pan once or twice, and when adding ingredients. Add the peas and dill and season. Cook for 10 minutes, or until the rice is almost cooked, adding more stock if necessary. Add the cod and mussels and cook for 3 minutes.

4 When all the liquid has been absorbed and you detect a faint toasty aroma coming from the rice, remove from the heat immediately. Cover with foil and let stand for 5 minutes. Garnish with dill and serve with lemon wedges.

seafood risotto

ingredients

SERVES 4

8 oz/225 g prepared raw shrimp, heads and shells reserved
2 garlic cloves, halved
1 lemon, sliced
8 oz/225 g live mussels*, scrubbed and debearded
8 oz/225 g live clams*, scrubbed
20 fl oz/625 ml/2½ cups water
4 oz/115 g butter
1 tbsp olive oil
1 onion, finely chopped
2 tbsp chopped fresh flat-leaf parsley
12 oz/350 g/1¾ cups Arborio rice
4 fl oz/125 ml/½ cup dry white wine
8 oz/225 g cleaned raw squid, cut into small pieces, or squid rings
4 tbsp Marsala
salt and pepper

* discard any mussels or clams that remain closed after cooking

method

1 Wrap the shrimp heads and shells in a square of cheesecloth and pound with a pestle. Put the wrapped shells and their liquid in a pan with the garlic, lemon, mussels, and clams. Add the water, cover, and bring to a boil over high heat. Cook, shaking the pan frequently, for 5 minutes until the shellfish have opened. Let cool, then shell and set aside. Strain the cooking liquid through a strainer lined with cheesecloth and add water to make 40 fl oz/ 1.25 liters/5 cups. Bring to a boil in a pan, then let simmer gently over low heat.

2 Melt 2 tablespoons of butter with the olive oil in a pan. Cook the onion and half the parsley over medium heat, stirring occasionally, until softened. Reduce the heat, stir in the rice, and cook, stirring, until the grains are translucent. Add the wine and cook, stirring, for 1 minute until reduced. Add the hot cooking liquid a ladleful at a time, stirring constantly, until all the liquid is absorbed and the rice is creamy.

3 Melt 2 oz/55 g of the remaining butter in a pan. Cook the squid, stirring frequently, for 3 minutes. Add the shrimp and cook for 2–3 minutes, until the squid is opaque and the shrimp have changed color. Add the Marsala, bring to a boil, and cook until the liquid has evaporated. Stir all the seafood into the rice, add the remaining butter and parsley, and season. Heat gently and serve at once.

springtime pasta

ingredients

SERVES 4

2 tbsp lemon juice
4 baby globe artichokes
7 tbsp olive oil
2 shallots, chopped finely
2 garlic cloves, chopped finely
2 tbsp chopped fresh flat-leaf parsley
2 tbsp chopped fresh mint
12 oz/350 g dried rigatoni or other tubular pasta
12 large raw shrimp, shelled
1 oz/25 g unsalted butter
salt and pepper

method

1 Fill a bowl with cold water and add the lemon juice. Prepare the artichokes one at a time. Cut off the stems and trim away any tough outer leaves. Cut across the tops of the leaves. Slice in half lengthwise and remove the central fibrous chokes, then cut lengthwise into 1/4-inch/5-mm thick slices. Immediately place the slices in the bowl of acidulated water to prevent discoloration.

2 Heat 5 tablespoons of the olive oil in a heavy-bottom skillet. Drain the artichoke slices and pat dry with paper towels. Add them to the skillet with the shallots, garlic, parsley, and mint, and cook over low heat, stirring frequently, for 10–12 minutes, or until tender.

3 Meanwhile, bring a large pan of lightly salted water to a boil. Add the pasta, bring back to a boil, and cook for 8–10 minutes, until tender but still firm to the bite.

4 Cut a slit along the back of each shrimp and remove and discard the dark vein. Melt the butter in a small skillet, cut the shrimp in half, and add them to the skillet. Cook, stirring occasionally, for 2–3 minutes, until they have changed color. Season with salt and pepper.

5 Drain the pasta and pour it into a bowl. Add the remaining olive oil and toss well. Add the artichoke mixture and the shrimp and toss again. Serve immediately.

linguine with anchovies, olives, & capers

ingredients

SERVES 4

3 tbsp olive oil
2 garlic cloves, finely chopped
10 canned anchovy fillets in oil, drained and chopped
5 oz/140 g/generous 3/4 cup black olives, pitted and chopped
1 tbsp capers, rinsed
1 lb/450 g plum tomatoes, peeled, seeded, and chopped
pinch of cayenne pepper
salt
14 oz/400 g dried linguine
2 tbsp chopped fresh flat-leaf parsley, to garnish

method

1 Heat the oil in a heavy-bottom pan over low heat, add the garlic, and cook, stirring frequently, for 2 minutes. Add the anchovies and mash them to a pulp with a fork. Add the olives, capers, and tomatoes and season with cayenne pepper. Cover and let simmer for 25 minutes.

2 Meanwhile, bring a pan of lightly salted water to a boil. Add the pasta, return to a boil, and cook for 8–10 minutes until tender but still firm to the bite. Drain the pasta and transfer to a warmed serving dish.

3 Spoon the anchovy sauce into the dish and toss the pasta using 2 large forks. Garnish with chopped parsley and serve at once.

vegetarian

Brightly colored vegetables, and taste-bud-tingling flavors such as olive oil, garlic, citrus fruits, and herbs, feature prominently in the Mediterranean diet, so although the various countries are not specifically vegetarian-friendly, there are plenty of dishes to keep a vegetarian happy! Choose one of the hearty main dishes, such as Eggplant Tagine with Polenta, Roasted Vegetable Moussaka, Zucchini & Cheese Gratin, Artichoke Paella, Spinach & Feta Pie, or Spanish Tortilla, and surround it with some of the wonderful side dishes—Oven-dried Tomatoes, Crispy Roasted Fennel, Parmesan Pumpkin, Spinach with Chickpeas, and a Roasted Bell Pepper Salad—for a satisfying and very appetizing vegetarian feast.

These dishes also make great accompaniments to meat or fish dishes, or can be served as part of an alfresco summer lunch or evening party. Roasted Summer Vegetables, Stuffed Zucchini with Walnuts & Feta, Roasted Red Bell Peppers with Provolone, Toasted Pine Nut & Vegetable Couscous, Greek Salad, and Tabbouleh would all look wonderful served in colorful bowls and arranged on a generously sized table covered in a cheerful cloth. The food will taste absolutely delicious and will certainly be a great talking point for your guests!

eggplant gratin

ingredients

SERVES 4

4 tbsp olive oil
2 onions, finely chopped
2 garlic cloves, very finely chopped
2 eggplants, thickly sliced
3 tbsp chopped fresh flat-leaf parsley
1/2 tsp dried thyme
salt and pepper
14 oz/400 g canned chopped tomatoes
6 oz/175 g mozzarella cheese, coarsely grated
6 tbsp freshly grated Parmesan cheese

method

1 Heat the oil in a skillet over medium heat. Add the onion and cook for 5 minutes, or until softened. Add the garlic and cook for a few seconds, or until just beginning to color. Using a slotted spoon, transfer the onion mixture to a plate. Cook the eggplant slices in batches in the same skillet until they are just lightly browned.

2 Arrange a layer of eggplant slices in a shallow ovenproof dish. Sprinkle with some of the parsley, thyme, salt, and pepper. Add a layer of onion, tomatoes, and mozzarella, sprinkling parsley, thyme, salt, and pepper over each layer.

3 Continue layering, finishing with a layer of eggplant slices. Sprinkle with the Parmesan cheese. Bake, uncovered, in a preheated oven, 400°F/200°C, for 20–30 minutes, or until the top is golden and the eggplants are tender. Serve hot.

eggplant tagine with cornmeal

ingredients

SERVES 4

1 eggplant, cut into 1/2-inch/1-cm cubes
3 tbsp olive oil
1 large onion, thinly sliced
1 carrot, diced
2 garlic cloves, chopped
4 oz/115 g mushrooms, sliced
2 tsp ground coriander
2 tsp cumin seeds
1 tsp chili powder
1 tsp ground turmeric
20 fl oz/600 ml/2 1/2 cups canned chopped tomatoes
10 fl oz/300 ml/1 1/4 cups vegetable stock
1 tbsp tomato paste
2 3/4 oz/75 g/scant 1/2 cup no-soak dried apricots, coarsely chopped
14 oz/400 g canned chickpeas, drained
2 tbsp fresh cilantro, to garnish

cornmeal

40 fl oz/1.25 liters/5 cups hot vegetable stock
7 oz/200 g/generous 1/4 cup instant cornmeal

method

1 Toss the eggplant in 1 tablespoon of the oil and arrange in a broiler pan. Cook under a broiler preheated to medium for 20 minutes, turning occasionally, until softened and starting to blacken around the edges—brush with more oil if the eggplant becomes too dry.

2 Heat the remaining oil in a large, heavy-bottom pan over medium heat. Add the onion and cook, stirring occasionally, for 8 minutes, or until soft and golden. Add the carrot, garlic, and mushrooms and cook for 5 minutes. Add the spices and cook, stirring constantly, for an additional minute.

3 Add the tomatoes and stock, stir well, then add the tomato paste. Bring to a boil, then reduce the heat and let simmer for 10 minutes, or until the sauce starts to thicken and reduce. Add the eggplant, apricots, and chickpeas, partially cover, and cook for an additional 10 minutes, stirring occasionally.

4 Meanwhile, to make the cornmeal, pour the hot stock into a pan and bring to a boil. Pour in the cornmeal in a steady stream, stirring constantly with a wooden spoon. Reduce the heat to low and cook for 1–2 minutes, or until the cornmeal thickens. Serve the tagine with the cornmeal, sprinkled with the fresh cilantro.

roasted vegetable moussaka

ingredients

SERVES 4–6

1 large eggplant , sliced thickly
2 medium zucchini, sliced thickly
2 onions, cut into small wedges
2 red bell peppers, cored, seeded and chopped coarsely
2 garlic cloves, chopped coarsely
5 tbsp olive oil
1 tbsp chopped fresh thyme
salt and pepper
2 eggs, beaten
10 fl oz/300 ml/1 1/4 cups strained plain yogurt
14 oz/400 g canned chopped tomatoes in juice
2 oz/55 g/1/3 cup feta cheese

method

1 Put the eggplant, zucchini, onions, bell peppers, and garlic in a roasting pan. Drizzle over the oil, toss together, and then sprinkle over the thyme and season with salt and pepper. Roast in a preheated oven, 425°F/ 220°C, for 30–35 minutes, turning the pan halfway through the cooking, until golden brown and tender.

2 Meanwhile, beat together the eggs and yogurt and season with salt and pepper. When the vegetables are cooked, reduce the oven temperature to 350°F/180°C.

3 Put half the vegetables in a layer in a large ovenproof dish. Spoon over the canned chopped tomatoes and their juice, then add the remaining vegetables. Pour over the yogurt mixture and crumble over the feta cheese. Bake in the oven for 45 minutes to 1 hour, until golden brown. Serve hot, warm, or cold.

roasted summer vegetables

ingredients

SERVES 4

2 tbsp olive oil
1 fennel bulb
2 red onions
2 beefsteak tomatoes
1 eggplant
2 zucchini
1 yellow bell pepper
1 red bell pepper
1 orange bell pepper
4 garlic cloves, peeled but left whole
4 fresh rosemary sprigs
pepper
crusty bread, to serve (optional)

method

1 Brush a large ovenproof dish with a little of the oil. Prepare the vegetables. Cut the fennel bulb, red onions, and tomatoes into wedges. Slice the eggplant and zucchini thickly, then seed all the bell peppers and cut into chunks. Arrange the vegetables in the dish and tuck the garlic cloves and rosemary sprigs among them. Drizzle with the remaining oil and season with pepper.

2 Roast the vegetables in a preheated oven, 400°F/200°C, for 10 minutes. Remove the dish from the oven and turn the vegetables over using a slotted spoon. Return the dish to the oven and roast for an additional 10–15 minutes, or until the vegetables are tender and starting to turn golden brown.

3 Serve the vegetables straight from the dish or transfer them to a warmed serving plate. For a vegetarian main course, serve with crusty bread, if you like.

rustic roasted ratatouille

ingredients

SERVES 4

$10^1/_2$ oz/300 g potatoes in their skins, scrubbed

7 oz/200 g eggplant, cut into $^1/_2$-inch/1-cm wedges

$4^1/_2$ oz/125 g red onion cut into $^1/_4$-inch/5-mm slices

7 oz/200 g seeded mixed bell peppers, sliced into $^1/_2$-inch/1-cm strips

6 oz/175 g zucchini, cut in half lengthwise, then into $^1/_2$-inch/1-cm slices

$4^1/_2$ oz/125 g cherry tomatoes

$3^1/_4$ oz/90 g cream cheese

1 tsp runny honey

pinch of smoked paprika

1 tsp chopped fresh parsley, to garnish

marinade

1 tsp vegetable oil

1 tbsp lemon juice

4 tbsp white wine

1 tsp sugar

2 tbsp chopped fresh basil

1 tsp finely chopped fresh rosemary

1 tbsp finely chopped fresh lemon thyme

$^1/_4$ tsp smoked paprika

method

1 Bake the potatoes in a preheated oven, 400°F/200°C, for 30 minutes, then remove and cut into wedges—the flesh should not be completely cooked.

2 To make the marinade, place all the ingredients in a bowl and blend with a hand-held electric blender until smooth, or use a food processor.

3 Put the potato wedges into a large bowl with the eggplant, onion, bell peppers, and zucchini, then pour over the marinade and mix thoroughly.

4 Arrange on a nonstick baking tray and roast in the oven, turning occasionally, for 25–30 minutes, or until golden brown and tender. Add the tomatoes for the last 5 minutes of the cooking time, just to split the skins and warm slightly.

5 Mix the cream cheese, honey, and paprika together in a bowl.

6 Serve the vegetables with the fromage frais mixture, and sprinkle with chopped parsley, to garnish.

stuffed zucchini with walnuts & feta

ingredients

SERVES 4

4 fat, medium zucchini
3 tbsp olive oil
1 onion, chopped finely
1 garlic clove, chopped finely
2 oz/55 g/$^1/_3$ cup feta cheese, crumbled
1 oz/25 g/$^1/_4$ cup walnut pieces, chopped
2 oz/55 g/1 cup white bread crumbs
1 egg, beaten
1 tsp chopped fresh dill
salt and pepper

method

1 Put the zucchini in a pan of boiling water, return to a boil, and then boil for 3 minutes. Drain, rinse under cold water, and drain again. Let cool.

2 When the zucchini are cool enough to handle, cut a thin strip off the top side of each one with a sharp knife. Using a teaspoon, carefully scoop out the flesh, leaving a shell to hold the stuffing. Chop the zucchini flesh.

3 Heat 2 tablespoons of the oil in a pan. Add the onion and garlic and fry for 5 minutes, until softened. Add the zucchini flesh and fry for 5 minutes, until the onion is golden brown. Remove from the heat and let cool slightly. Stir in the cheese then the walnuts, bread crumbs, egg, dill, salt, and pepper.

4 Use the stuffing to fill the zucchini shells, and place side by side in an ovenproof dish. Drizzle over the remaining oil.

5 Cover the dish with foil and bake in a preheated oven, 375°F/190°C, for 30 minutes. Remove the foil and bake for another 10–15 minutes or until golden brown. Serve hot.

zucchini & cheese gratin

ingredients

SERVES 4–6

2 oz/55 g unsalted butter, plus extra for greasing
6 zucchini, sliced
salt and pepper
2 tbsp chopped fresh tarragon or a mixture of mint, tarragon, and flat-leaf parsley
7 oz/200 g/2 cups Gruyère or Parmesan cheese, grated
4fl oz/125 ml/1/2 cup milk
4fl oz/125 ml/1/2 cup heavy cream
2 eggs
freshly grated nutmeg

method

1 Melt the butter in a large sauté pan or skillet over medium-high heat. Add the zucchini and sauté for 4–6 minutes, turning the slices over occasionally, until colored on both sides. Remove from the pan and drain on paper towels, then season with salt and pepper.

2 Spread half the zucchini over the bottom of a greased ovenproof serving dish. Sprinkle with half the herbs and 2 oz/55 g/3/4 cup of the cheese. Repeat these layers once more.

3 Mix the milk, cream, and eggs together and season with nutmeg, salt, and pepper. Pour this liquid over the zucchini, then sprinkle the top with the remaining cheese.

4 Bake the gratin in a preheated oven, 350°F/180°C, for 35–45 minutes, or until it is set in the center and golden brown. Remove from the oven and let stand for 5 minutes before serving straight from the dish.

paella de verduras

ingredients

SERVES 4–6

- 1/2 tsp saffron threads
- 2 tbsp hot water
- 3 tbsp olive oil
- 1 large onion, chopped
- 2 garlic cloves, crushed
- 1 tsp paprika
- 8 oz/225 g tomatoes, peeled and cut into wedges
- 1 red bell pepper, halved and seeded, then broiled, peeled, and sliced
- 1 green bell pepper, halved and seeded, then broiled, peeled, and sliced
- 15 oz/425 g canned chickpeas, drained
- 12 oz/350 g/generous 1 1/2 cups medium-grain paella rice
- 42 fl oz/1.3 liters/5 1/4 cups simmering vegetable stock
- 2 oz/55 g/3/8 cup shelled peas
- 5 1/2 oz/150 g fresh asparagus spears, blanched
- 1 tbsp chopped fresh flat-leaf parsley, plus extra to garnish
- salt and pepper
- 1 lemon, cut into wedges, to serve

method

1 Put the saffron threads and water in a small bowl and let infuse for a few minutes.

2 Meanwhile, heat the oil in a paella pan and cook the onion over medium heat, stirring, for 2–3 minutes, or until softened. Add the garlic, paprika, and saffron and its soaking liquid and cook, stirring, for 1 minute. Add the tomatoes, bell peppers, and chickpeas and cook, stirring, for an additional 2 minutes.

3 Add the rice and cook, stirring constantly, for 1 minute, or until glossy and coated. Pour in most of the hot stock and bring to a boil. Reduce the heat and let simmer, uncovered, for 10 minutes. Do not stir during cooking, but shake the pan once or twice. Add the peas, asparagus, and parsley and season with salt and pepper. Shake the pan and cook for an additional 10–15 minutes, or until the rice grains are plump and cooked. Pour in a little more hot stock if necessary, then shake the pan to spread the liquid through the paella.

4 When all the liquid has been absorbed and you detect a faint toasty aroma coming from the rice, remove from the heat immediately to prevent burning. Cover the pan with foil and let stand for 5 minutes. Sprinkle over chopped parsley to garnish and serve direct from the pan, with the lemon wedges for squeezing over the rice.

artichoke paella

ingredients

SERVES 4–6

- 1/2 tsp saffron threads
- 2 tbsp hot water
- 3 tbsp olive oil
- 1 large onion, chopped
- 1 zucchini, coarsely chopped
- 2 garlic cloves, crushed
- 1/4 tsp cayenne pepper
- 8 oz/225 g tomatoes, peeled and cut into wedges
- 15 oz/425 g canned chickpeas, drained
- 15 oz/425 g canned artichokes hearts, drained and coarsely sliced
- 12 oz/350 g/generous 1 1/2 cups medium-grain paella rice
- 42 fl oz/1.3 liters/5 1/4 cups simmering vegetable stock
- 5 1/2 oz/150 g green beans, blanched
- salt and pepper
- 1 lemon, cut into wedges, to serve

method

1 Put the saffron threads and water in a small bowl and let infuse for a few minutes.

2 Meanwhile, heat the oil in a paella pan and cook the onion and zucchini over medium heat, stirring, for 2–3 minutes, or until softened. Add the garlic, cayenne pepper, and saffron and its soaking liquid and cook, stirring constantly, for 1 minute. Add the tomato wedges, chickpeas, and artichokes and cook, stirring, for an additional 2 minutes.

3 Add the rice and cook, stirring constantly, for 1 minute, or until the rice is glossy and coated. Pour in most of the hot stock and bring to a boil, then let simmer, uncovered, for 10 minutes. Do not stir during cooking, but shake the pan once or twice. Add the green beans and season. Shake the pan and cook for an additional 10–15 minutes, or until the rice grains are plump and cooked. If the liquid is absorbed too quickly, pour in a little more hot stock, then shake the pan to spread the liquid through the paella.

4 When all the liquid has been absorbed and you detect a faint toasty aroma coming from the rice, remove from the heat immediately to prevent burning. Cover the pan with foil and let stand for 5 minutes. Serve direct from the pan with the lemon wedges to squeeze over the rice.

provolone cheese & vegetable kabobs

ingredients

SERVES 4

kabobs

8 oz/225 g Provolone cheese
12 white mushrooms
8 pearl onions
12 cherry tomatoes
2 zucchini, cut into small chunks
1 red bell pepper, seeded and cut into small chunks
chopped fresh cilantro, to garnish
freshly cooked rice or fresh mixed salad greens and fresh crusty bread, to serve

marinade

4 tbsp extra-virgin olive oil
2 tbsp balsamic vinegar
2 garlic cloves, finely chopped
1 tbsp chopped fresh cilantro
salt and pepper

method

1 If using wooden skewers, soak them in cold water for 30 minutes before use.

2 Put the oil, vinegar, garlic, and cilantro into a large bowl. Season with salt and pepper and mix until well combined.

3 Cut the Provolone cheese into bite-size cubes. Thread the cubes onto skewers, alternating them with whole white mushrooms, pearl onions, and cherry tomatoes, and zucchini and red bell pepper chunks. When the skewers are full (leave a small space at either end), transfer them to the bowl, and turn them in the marinade until they are well coated. Cover with plastic wrap and place in the refrigerator to marinate for at least 2 hours.

4 When the skewers are thoroughly marinated, grill them over hot coals for 5–10 minutes, or until they are cooked to your taste, turning frequently, and basting with the remaining marinade. Arrange the skewers on a bed of freshly cooked rice or fresh mixed salad greens, garnish with cilantro leaves, and serve with fresh crusty bread.

roasted red bell peppers with provolone

ingredients

SERVES 6

6 small red bell peppers
2 tbsp olive oil, plus extra for oiling
3 garlic cloves, sliced thinly
9 oz/250 g Provolone or Feta cheese, sliced thinly
12 fresh mint leaves
grated rind and juice of 1 lemon
1 tbsp chopped fresh thyme
3 tbsp pine nuts
pepper

method

1 Cut the bell peppers in half lengthwise and remove the cores and seeds. Rub the skins of the bell peppers with a little of the oil, then arrange the bell peppers, skin-side down, on a large oiled cookie sheet.

2 Scatter half the garlic into the bell peppers. Add the cheese, then the mint leaves, lemon rind, remaining garlic, thyme, pine nuts, and pepper. Drizzle over the remaining oil and the lemon juice.

3 Roast the bell peppers in a preheated oven, 400°F/200°C, for 30 minutes, until tender and beginning to char around the edges. Serve warm.

paella-stuffed mediterranean peppers

ingredients

SERVES 4

$1/2$ tsp saffron threads
2 tbsp hot water
3 tbsp olive oil
1 zucchini, diced
$5\frac{1}{2}$ oz/150 g white mushrooms
2 scallions, diced
2 garlic cloves, crushed
1 tsp paprika
$1/4$ tsp cayenne pepper
9 oz/250 g canned red kidney beans (drained weight)
8 oz/225 g tomatoes, peeled and chopped
13 oz/375 g/generous $1\frac{1}{2}$ cups paella rice
42 fl oz/1.2 liters/$5\frac{1}{4}$ cups simmering vegetable stock
4 oz/125 g/scant $1/2$ cup peas
1 tbsp chopped fresh flat-leaf parsley, plus extra to garnish
salt and pepper
4 large red bell peppers, tops cut off and set aside and seeds removed
$3\frac{1}{2}$ oz/100 g Manchego or Parmesan cheese, grated

method

1 Put the saffron threads and water in a bowl and let infuse. Meanwhile, heat the oil in a paella pan over medium heat and cook the zucchini, stirring, for 3 minutes. Add the mushrooms and scallions and cook, stirring, until softened. Add the garlic, paprika, cayenne pepper, and saffron and its soaking liquid and cook, stirring, for 1 minute. Add the beans and tomatoes and cook, stirring, for 2 minutes.

2 Add the rice and cook, stirring, for 1 minute to coat. Add most of the stock and bring to a boil, then let simmer, uncovered, for 10 minutes. Do not stir during cooking, but shake the pan once or twice. Add the peas and parsley, season, and shake the pan. Cook for 10–15 minutes, or until the rice grains are cooked. When all the liquid has been absorbed, remove from the heat. Cover with foil and let stand for 5 minutes.

3 Blanch the red bell peppers and their tops in a pan of boiling water for 2 minutes. Drain and pat dry with paper towels. Spoon a little cheese into each, then fill with paella and top with the remaining cheese. Replace the tops. Wrap each bell pepper in foil, then stand in an ovenproof dish and bake in a preheated oven, 350°F/180°C, for 25–30 minutes.

oven-dried tomatoes

ingredients

SERVES 4

- 2 lb 4 oz/1 kg large, juicy full-flavored tomatoes
- sea salt
- 1 lb 2 oz/500 g Buffalo Mozzarella, sliced
- extra-virgin olive oil for drizzling
- pepper
- basil leaves, to garnish

method

1 Using a sharp knife, cut each of the tomatoes into fourths lengthwise. Using a teaspoon, scoop out the seeds and discard. If the tomatoes are large, cut each fourth in half lengthwise again.

2 Sprinkle sea salt in a roasting pan and arrange the tomato slices, skin side down, on top. Roast in a preheated oven, 250°F/120°C, for 2^{1}/2 hours, or until the edges are just beginning to look charred and the flesh is dry but still pliable. The exact roasting time and yield will depend on the size and juiciness of the tomatoes. Check the tomatoes at 30-minute intervals after 1^{1}/2 hours.

3 Remove the dried tomatoes from the roasting pan and let cool completely. Serve with slices of buffalo mozzarella, drizzled with olive oil and sprinkled with pepper and basil leaves.

toasted pine nut & vegetable couscous

ingredients

SERVES 4

4 oz/115 g/generous 1/2 cup dried green lentils

2 oz/55 g/3/8 cup pine nuts

1 tbsp olive oil

1 onion, diced

2 garlic cloves, crushed

10 oz/280 g zucchini, sliced

9 oz/250 g tomatoes, chopped

14 oz/400 g canned artichoke hearts, drained and cut in half lengthwise

9 oz/250 g/generous 1 1/4 cups couscous

16 fl oz/500 ml/2 cups vegetable stock

3 tbsp torn fresh basil leaves, plus extra leaves to garnish

pepper

method

1 Put the lentils into a pan with plenty of cold water, bring to a boil, and boil rapidly for 10 minutes. Reduce the heat, cover, and let simmer for 15 minutes, or until tender.

2 Meanwhile, preheat the broiler to medium. Spread the pine nuts out in a single layer on a cookie sheet and toast under the preheated broiler, turning to brown evenly—watch constantly because they brown very quickly. Tip the pine nuts into a small dish and set aside.

3 Heat the oil in a skillet over medium heat, add the onion, garlic, and zucchini and cook, stirring frequently, for 8–10 minutes, or until tender and the zucchini have browned slightly. Add the tomatoes and artichoke halves and heat through thoroughly for 5 minutes.

4 Meanwhile, put the couscous into a heatproof bowl. Bring the stock to a boil in a pan and pour over the couscous, cover, and let stand for 10 minutes until the couscous absorbs the stock and becomes tender.

5 Drain the lentils and stir into the couscous. Stir in the torn basil leaves and season well with pepper. Transfer the couscous to a warmed serving dish and spoon over the cooked vegetables. Sprinkle the pine nuts over the top, garnish with basil leaves, and serve at once.

parmesan pumpkin

ingredients

SERVES 6

2 tbsp virgin olive oil
1 onion, chopped finely
1 garlic clove, chopped finely
14 fl oz/425 ml/$1^3/_4$ cups strained tomatoes
10 fresh basil leaves, shredded
2 tbsp chopped fresh flat-leaf parsley
1 tsp sugar
salt and pepper
2 eggs, beaten lightly
2 oz/55 g/$^1/_2$ cup dried, white bread crumbs
$3^1/_2$ lb/1.6 kg pumpkin, peeled, seeded, and sliced
2 oz/55 g butter, plus extra for greasing
2 oz/55 g/$^1/_2$ cup freshly grated Parmesan cheese

method

1 Heat the olive oil in a large pan, add the onion and garlic, and cook over low heat for 5 minutes, until softened. Stir in the strained tomatoes, basil, parsley, and sugar, and season with salt and pepper. Let simmer for 10–15 minutes, until thickened.

2 Meanwhile, put the beaten eggs in a shallow dish and spread out the bread crumbs in another shallow dish. Dip the slices of pumpkin first in the egg, then in the bread crumbs to coat, shaking off any excess.

3 Grease a large ovenproof dish with butter. Melt the butter in a large, heavy-bottom skillet. Add the pumpkin slices, in batches, and cook until browned all over. Transfer the slices to the dish. Pour the sauce over them and sprinkle with the Parmesan.

4 Bake in a preheated oven, 350°F/180°C, for 30 minutes, until the cheese is bubbling and golden. Serve immediately.

crispy roasted fennel

ingredients

SERVES 4–6

3 large fennel bulbs
4 tbsp olive oil
finely grated rind and juice of 1 small lemon
1 garlic clove, chopped finely
2 oz/55 g/1 cup fresh white bread crumbs
salt and pepper

method

1 Trim the fennel bulbs, reserving the green feathery fronds, and cut into fourths. Cook the bulbs in a large pan of boiling salted water for 5 minutes until just tender, then drain well.

2 Heat 2 tablespoons of the olive oil in a small roasting pan or skillet with a flameproof handle, add the fennel, and turn to coat in the oil. Drizzle over the lemon juice. Roast the fennel in a preheated oven, 400°F/200°C, for about 35 minutes, until beginning to brown.

3 Meanwhile, heat the remaining oil in a skillet. Add the garlic and fry for 1 minute, until lightly browned. Add the bread crumbs and fry for about 5 minutes, stirring frequently, until crisp. Remove from the heat and stir in the lemon rind, reserved snipped fennel fronds, salt, and pepper.

4 When the fennel is cooked, sprinkle the bread crumb mixture over the top and return to the oven for another 5 minutes. Serve hot.

spinach with chickpeas

ingredients

SERVES 4–6

2 tbsp olive oil
1 large garlic clove, cut in half
1 medium onion, chopped finely
1/2 tsp cumin
pinch cayenne pepper
pinch turmeric
1 lb 12 oz/800 g canned chickpeas, drained and rinsed
18 oz/500 g baby spinach leaves, rinsed and shaken dry
2 pimientos del piquillo, drained and sliced
salt and pepper

method

1 Heat the oil in a large, lidded skillet over medium-high heat. Add the garlic and cook for 2 minutes, or until golden, but not brown. Remove with a slotted spoon and discard.

2 Add the onion and cumin, cayenne and turmeric and cook, stirring, for about 5 minutes until soft. Add the chickpeas and stir around until they are lightly colored with the turmeric and cayenne.

3 Stir in the spinach with just the water clinging to its leaves. Cover and cook for 4–5 minutes until wilted. Uncover, stir in the pimientos del piquillo and continue cooking, stirring gently, until all the liquid evaporates. Season with salt and pepper and serve.

spinach & feta pie

ingredients

SERVES 6

2 tbsp olive oil
1 large onion, chopped finely
2 lb 4 oz/1 kg fresh young spinach leaves, washed or 1 lb 2 oz/500 g frozen spinach, thawed
4 tbsp chopped fresh flat-leaf parsley
2 tbsp chopped fresh dill
3 eggs, beaten
7 oz/200 g feta cheese
salt and pepper
3½ oz/100 g butter
8 oz/225 g filo pastry (work with one sheet at a time and keep the remaining sheets covered with a damp dish towel)

method

1 To make the filling, heat the oil in a pan, add the onion, and fry until softened. Add the fresh spinach if using, with only the water clinging to the leaves after washing, or the frozen spinach, and cook for 2–5 minutes, until just wilted. Remove from the heat and let cool.

2 When the mixture has cooled, add the parsley, dill, and eggs. Crumble in the cheese, season with salt and pepper, and mix well.

3 Melt the butter and use a little to grease a deep 12 x 8-inch/30 x 20-cm metal baking pan. Cut the pastry sheets in half widthwise. Take 1 sheet of pastry and use it to line the base and sides of the pan. Brush the pastry with a little of the melted butter. Repeat with half of the pastry sheets, brushing each one with butter.

4 Spread the filling over the pastry, then top with the remaining pastry sheets, brushing each with butter and tucking down the edges. Using a sharp knife, score the top layers of the pastry into 6 squares.

5 Bake in a preheated oven, 375°F/190°C, for about 40 minutes, until golden brown. Serve hot or cold.

spanish tortilla

ingredients

MAKES 8–10 SLICES

4 fl oz/125 ml/$^{1}/_{2}$ cup olive oil
1 lb 5 oz/600 g potatoes, peeled and thinly sliced
1 large onion, thinly sliced
6 large eggs
salt and pepper
fresh flat-leaf parsley sprigs, to garnish

method

1 Heat a 10-inch/25-cm skillet over high heat. Add the oil and heat. Reduce the heat, then add the potatoes and onion and cook for 15–20 minutes, until the potatoes are tender.

2 Beat the eggs in a large bowl and season generously. Drain the potatoes and onion through a strainer over a heatproof bowl to reserve the oil. Very gently stir the vegetables into the eggs. Let stand for 10 minutes.

3 Wipe out the skillet, add 4 tablespoons of the reserved oil, and heat over medium-high heat. Add the egg mixture and press the potatoes and onions into an even layer.

4 Cook for about 5 minutes, shaking the skillet occasionally, until the bottom is set. Use a spatula to loosen the side of the tortilla. Place a large plate over the top and carefully invert the skillet and plate together so the tortilla drops onto the plate.

5 Add 1 tablespoon of the remaining reserved oil to the skillet and swirl around. Carefully slide the tortilla back into the skillet, cooked side up. Run the spatula round the tortilla and continue cooking for 3 minutes, or until the eggs are set and the bottom is golden brown. Remove from the heat and slide the tortilla onto a plate. Let stand for at least 5 minutes before cutting. Garnish with parsley sprigs and serve warm or at room temperature.

roasted bell pepper salad

ingredients

SERVES 8

3 red bell peppers
3 yellow bell peppers
5 tbsp Spanish extra-virgin olive oil
2 tbsp dry sherry vinegar or lemon juice
2 garlic cloves, crushed
pinch of sugar
salt and pepper
1 tbsp capers
8 small black Spanish olives
2 tbsp chopped fresh marjoram, plus extra sprigs to garnish

method

1 Place the bell peppers on a wire rack or broiler pan and cook under a broiler preheated to high for 10 minutes, until their skins have blackened and blistered, turning them frequently.

2 Remove the roasted bell peppers from the heat, and either put them in a bowl and immediately cover tightly with a clean, damp dish towel, or put them in a plastic bag. The steam helps to soften the skins and makes it easier to remove them. Let the peppers stand for about 15 minutes, until they are cool enough to handle.

3 Holding one bell pepper at a time over a clean bowl, use a sharp knife to make a small hole in the base and gently squeeze out the juices and reserve them. Still holding the bell pepper over the bowl, carefully peel off the blackened skin with your fingers or a knife and discard it. Cut the bell peppers in half and remove the stem, core, and seeds, then cut each bell pepper into neat thin strips. Arrange the bell pepper strips on a serving dish.

4 To the reserved pepper juices add the olive oil, sherry vinegar, garlic, sugar, salt, and pepper. Whisk together until combined. Drizzle the dressing evenly over the salad.

5 Sprinkle the capers, olives, and chopped marjoram over the salad, garnish with marjoram sprigs, and serve at room temperature.

greek salad

ingredients

SERVES 4

4 tomatoes, cut into wedges
1 onion, sliced
1/2 cucumber, sliced
8 oz/225g/1 1/3 cups kalamata olives, pitted
8 oz/225 g feta cheese, cubed (drained weight)
2 tbsp fresh cilantro leaves
fresh flat-leaf parsley, to garnish
pita bread, to serve

dressing

5 tbsp extra virgin olive oil
2 tbsp white wine vinegar
1 tbsp lemon juice
1/2 tsp sugar
1 tbsp chopped fresh cilantro
salt and pepper

method

1 To make the dressing, place the oil, vinegar, lemon juice, sugar, and cilantro in a large bowl. Season with salt and pepper and mix together well.

2 Add the tomatoes, onion, cucumber, olives, feta cheese, and cilantro. Toss all the ingredients together, then divide among individual serving bowls. Garnish with fresh parsley and serve with pita bread.

tabbouleh

ingredients

SERVES 4

- 6 oz/175 g/scant 1 cup bulgur wheat
- 3 tbsp extra-virgin olive oil
- 4 tbsp lemon juice
- salt and pepper
- 4 scallions
- 1 green bell pepper, seeded and sliced
- 4 tomatoes, chopped
- 2 tbsp chopped fresh parsley
- 2 tbsp chopped fresh mint
- 8 black olives, pitted
- chopped fresh mint, to garnish

method

1 Place the bulgur wheat in a large bowl and add enough cold water to cover. Let stand for 30 minutes, or until the wheat has doubled in size. Drain well and press out as much liquid as possible. Spread out the wheat on paper towels to dry.

2 Place the wheat in a serving bowl. Mix the olive oil and lemon juice together in a pitcher and season with salt and pepper. Pour the lemon mixture over the wheat and let marinate for 1 hour.

3 Using a sharp knife, finely chop the scallions, then add to the salad with the green bell pepper, tomatoes, parsley, and mint and toss lightly to mix. Top the salad with the olives and garnish with the chopped mint. Serve immediately.

baking & desserts

The secret of the success of the Mediterranean diet, and its contribution toward a long and healthy life, is perhaps partly a question of balance. Alongside all the fantastic ingredients that combine to promote a healthy heart, there is still room for more than a little indulgence!

Bread is baked fresh daily and eaten with every meal—Olive & Sun-dried Tomato Bread and Mini Focaccia make an excellent accompaniment to everything from a simple broiled fish dish to a rich, meaty stew, while Walnut Cheese Wafers make a protein-packed partner to salads.

And for that sweet tooth? There's plenty to satisfy it here! Mediterranean cakes and desserts make wonderful use of regional ingredients, such as nuts and citrus fruits—try Moroccan Orange & Almond Cake, Almond Tart, or Lemon Tart. Ice creams and chilled desserts are a refreshing foil to the relentless summer sun—Pistachio Ice Cream, Sicilian Ice Cream Cake, and Lemon Sherbet with Cava are all lovely, and the Frozen Almond Cream is divine.

And if that healthy heart is your main concern, the Baked Apricots with Honey and Broiled Honey Figs with Zabaglione are a Mediterranean treat for you.

olive & sun-dried tomato bread

ingredients

SERVES 4

- 14 oz/400 g/generous $2\frac{3}{4}$ cups all-purpose flour, plus extra for dusting
- 1 tsp salt
- 1 sachet active dry yeast
- 1 tsp brown sugar
- 1 tbsp chopped fresh thyme
- 7 fl oz/200 ml/scant 1 cup warm water (heated to 122°F/50°C)
- 4 tbsp olive oil, plus extra for oiling
- $1\frac{3}{4}$ oz/50 g/$\frac{1}{3}$ cup black olives, pitted and sliced
- $1\frac{3}{4}$ oz/50 g$\frac{1}{3}$ cup green olives, pitted and sliced
- $3\frac{1}{2}$ oz/100 g/$\frac{3}{8}$ cup sun-dried tomatoes in oil, drained and sliced
- 1 egg yolk, beaten

method

1 Place the flour, salt, and yeast in a bowl and mix together, then stir in the sugar and thyme. Make a well in the center. Slowly stir in enough water and oil to make a dough. Mix in the olives and sun-dried tomatoes. Knead the dough for 5 minutes, then form it into a ball. Brush a bowl with oil, add the dough, and cover with plastic wrap. Let rise in a warm place for about $1\frac{1}{2}$ hours, or until it has doubled in size.

2 Dust a cookie sheet with flour. Knead the dough lightly, then cut into two halves and shape into ovals or circles. Place them on the cookie sheet, cover with plastic wrap, and let rise again in a warm place for 45 minutes, or until they have doubled in size.

3 Make 3 shallow diagonal cuts on the top of each piece of dough. Brush with the egg. Bake in a preheated oven, 400°F/200°C, for 40 minutes, or until cooked through—the loaves should be golden on top and sound hollow when tapped on the bottom. Transfer to wire racks to cool.

mini focaccia

ingredients

SERVES 4

12 oz/350 g/2 1/4 cups strong white flour, plus extra for dusting
1/2 tsp salt
1/6-oz/7-g package active dry yeast
2 tbsp olive oil, plus extra for oiling
8 fl oz/250 ml/scant 1 1/4 cups lukewarm water
3 1/2 oz/100 g/generous 1/2 cup pitted green or black olives, halved

topping

2 red onions, sliced
2 tbsp olive oil
1 tsp sea salt
1 tbsp thyme leaves

method

1 Sift the flour and salt into a large bowl. Stir in the yeast, pour in the oil and water and mix to form a dough. Turn the dough out onto a floured counter and knead for 5 minutes. Alternatively, use an electric mixer with a dough hook.

2 Place the dough in an oiled bowl, cover, and let stand in a warm place for 1–1 1/2 hours, or until doubled in size. Punch down the dough by kneading it again for 1–2 minutes.

3 Knead half of the olives into the dough. Divide the dough into fourths and shape the fourths into circles. Place them on an oiled cookie sheet and push your fingers into the dough to create a dimpled effect.

4 To make the topping, sprinkle the red onions and remaining olives over the circles. Drizzle the oil over the top and sprinkle with the sea salt and thyme leaves. Cover and let stand for 30 minutes.

5 Bake in a preheated oven, 375°F/190°C, for 20–25 minutes, or until the focaccia are golden. Transfer to a wire rack and let cool before serving.

walnut cheese wafers

ingredients

MAKES ABOUT 38

$1^{1}/_{2}$ oz/40 g/$^{1}/_{4}$ cup walnut pieces
4 oz/115 g/$^{3}/_{4}$ cup all-purpose flour, plus extra for dusting
salt and pepper
4 oz/115 g butter
4 oz/115 g feta cheese
beaten egg, for glazing

method

1 Put the walnuts in a food processor and chop finely. Remove from the processor and set aside.

2 Add the flour, salt, and pepper to the processor bowl. Cut the butter into small pieces, add to the flour, and mix, in short bursts, until the mixture resembles fine bread crumbs. Coarsely grate in the cheese, add the reserved walnuts, and mix quickly to form a dough.

3 Turn the mixture onto a lightly floured counter and roll out thinly. Using a $2^{1}/_{4}$-inch/6-cm round cookie cutter, cut the dough into rounds and place on cookie sheets. Brush the tops with beaten egg.

4 Bake the wafers in a preheated oven, 375°F/190°C, for about 10 minutes, until golden. Cool on a wire rack.

5 Store in an airtight tin.

greek shortbread cookies

ingredients

MAKES 24

8 oz/225 g butter, softened
2 oz/55 g/1/2 cup confectioners' sugar
1 egg yolk
1 tbsp ouzo or brandy
12 oz/350 g/2 1/2 cups all-purpose flour
4 oz/115 g/1 cup ground almonds
confectioners' sugar, for dredging

method

1 Put the butter and confectioners' sugar in a large bowl and beat until pale and fluffy. Beat in the egg yolk and ouzo or brandy and then the flour and almonds to form a soft, firm dough. Using your hands, quickly knead the mixture together.

2 Cut the dough into 24 pieces. Roll each piece into a ball and then into a sausage shape measuring about 3 inches/7.5 cm long. Place the sausage over one finger and press down on the ends to form a plump moon shape. Place on cookie sheets, allowing room for them to spread slightly.

3 Bake in a preheated oven, 350°F/180°C, for 15 minutes, until firm to the touch and light golden brown. Meanwhile, sift a layer of confectioners' sugar into a large roasting pan.

4 When baked, allow the cookies to cool slightly then place in the pan in a single layer, as close together as possible. Sift confectioners' sugar generously on top and let cool for 3–4 hours. Store them in an airtight tin with any remaining confectioners' sugar, so that the cookies remain coated.

almond cookies

ingredients

MAKES ABOUT 60

- $5^1/_2$ oz/150 g butter, at room temperature, plus extra for greasing
- $5^1/_2$ oz/150 g/generous $^3/_4$ cup superfine sugar
- 4 oz/115 g/generous $^3/_4$ cup all-purpose flour
- 1 oz/25 g/generous $^1/_4$ cup ground almonds
- pinch of salt
- $2^3/_4$ oz/75 g/generous $^1/_2$ cup blanched almonds, toasted lightly and chopped finely
- finely grated rind of 1 large lemon
- 4 medium egg whites

method

1 Put the butter and sugar into a bowl and beat until light and fluffy. Sift over the flour, ground almonds, and salt, tipping in any ground almonds left in the strainer. Use a large metal spoon to fold in the chopped almonds and lemon rind.

2 In a separate, spotlessly clean bowl, whisk the egg whites until soft peaks form. Fold the egg whites into the almond mixture.

3 Drop small teaspoonfuls of the cookie mixture onto one or more well-greased cookie sheets, spacing them well apart. (You might need to cook in batches.) Bake in a preheated oven, 350°F/180°C, for 15–20 minutes until the cookies are golden brown on the edges. Transfer to a wire rack to cool completely. Continue baking until all the mixture is used. Store in an airtight container for up to 1 week.

baklava

ingredients

SERVES 4

- $5\frac{1}{2}$ oz/150 g/1 cup shelled pistachio nuts, finely chopped
- $2\frac{3}{4}$ oz/75 g/$\frac{1}{2}$ cup toasted hazelnuts, finely chopped
- $2\frac{3}{4}$ oz/75 g/$\frac{1}{2}$ cup blanched hazelnuts, finely chopped
- grated rind of 1 lemon
- 1 tbsp brown sugar
- 1 tsp ground mixed spice
- $5\frac{1}{2}$ oz/150 g butter, melted, plus extra for greasing
- 9 oz/250 g (about 16 sheets) frozen filo pastry, thawed
- 8 fl oz/250 ml/generous 1 cup water
- 2 tbsp clear honey
- 1 tbsp lemon juice
- $10\frac{1}{2}$ oz/300 g/$1\frac{1}{2}$ cups superfine sugar
- $\frac{1}{2}$ tsp ground cinnamon

method

1 Place the nuts, lemon rind, brown sugar, and mixed spice in a bowl and mix well. Grease a round cake pan, 7 inches/18 cm in diameter and 2 inches/5 cm deep, with butter. Cut the whole stack of filo sheets to the size of the tin, then keep the rounds covered with a damp dish towel.

2 Lay one round on the base of the pan and brush with melted butter. Add another 6 rounds on top, brushing between each layer with melted butter. Spread over one-third of the nut mixture, then add 3 rounds of buttered filo. Spread over another third of the nut mixture then top with 3 more rounds of buttered filo. Spread over the remaining nut mixture and add the last 3 rounds of buttered filo. Cut into wedges, then bake in a preheated oven, 325°F/160°C, for 1 hour.

3 Meanwhile, place the water, honey, lemon juice, superfine sugar, and cinnamon in a pan. Bring to a boil, stirring. Reduce the heat and let simmer, without stirring, for 15 minutes, then remove from the heat and let cool. Remove the baklava from the oven, pour over the syrup and let set before serving.

moroccan orange & almond cake

ingredients

MAKES 1 X 8-INCH/20-CM CAKE

- 1 orange
- 4 oz/115 g butter, softened, plus extra for greasing
- 4 oz/115 g/generous 1/2 cup golden superfine sugar
- 2 eggs, beaten
- 6 oz/175 g/scant 1 cup semolina
- 3 1/2 oz/100 g/generous 1 cup ground almonds
- 1 1/2 tsp baking powder
- confectioners' sugar, for dusting
- strained plain yogurt, to serve

syrup

- 10 fl oz/300 ml/1 1/4 cups orange juice
- 4 3/4 oz/130 g/2/3 cup superfine sugar
- 8 cardamom pods, crushed

method

1 Grate the rind from the orange, reserving some for the decoration, and squeeze the juice from one half. Place the butter, orange rind, and superfine sugar in a bowl and beat together until light and fluffy. Gradually beat in the eggs.

2 In a separate bowl, mix the semolina, ground almonds, and baking powder, then fold into the creamed mixture with the orange juice. Spoon the batter into a greased and base-lined 8-inch/20-cm cake pan and bake in a preheated oven, 350°F/180°C, for 30–40 minutes, or until well risen and a skewer inserted into the center comes out clean. Let cool in the pan for 10 minutes.

3 To make the syrup, place the orange juice, sugar, and cardamom pods in a pan over low heat and stir until the sugar has dissolved. Bring to a boil and let simmer for 4 minutes, or until syrupy.

4 Turn the cake out into a deep serving dish. Using a skewer, make holes all over the surface of the warm cake. Strain the syrup into a separate bowl and spoon three-fourths of it over the cake, then let stand for 30 minutes. Dust the cake with confectioners' sugar and cut into slices. Serve with the remaining syrup drizzled around, accompanied by strained plain yogurt decorated with the reserved orange rind.

almond tart

ingredients

MAKES 1 X 10-INCH/25-CM TART

pie dough

10 oz/280 g/2 cups all-purpose flour
$5^1/_2$ oz/150 g generous $^3/_4$ cup superfine sugar
1 tsp finely grated lemon rind
pinch of salt
$5^1/_2$ oz/150 g unsalted butter, chilled and cut into small dice, plus extra for greasing
1 medium egg, beaten lightly
1 tbsp chilled water

filling

6 oz/175 g unsalted butter, at room temperature
6 oz/175 g/generous $^3/_4$ cup superfine sugar
3 large eggs
6 oz/175 g/generous $1^1/_2$ cups finely ground almonds
2 tsp all-purpose flour
1 tbsp finely grated orange rind
$^1/_2$ tsp almond extract
confectioners' sugar, to decorate
sour cream (optional), to serve

method

1 To make the pie dough, put the flour, sugar, lemon rind, and salt in a bowl. Rub or cut in the butter until the mixture resembles fine bread crumbs. Combine the egg and water, then slowly pour into the flour, stirring with a fork until a coarse mass forms. Shape into a ball and let chill for at least 1 hour.

2 Roll out the pie dough on a lightly floured counter until $^1/_8$ inch/3 mm thick. Use to line a greased 10-inch/25-cm tart pan. Return to the refrigerator for at least 15 minutes, then cover the pastry shell with foil and fill with pie weights or dried beans. Place in a preheated oven, 425°F/220°C, and bake for 12 minutes. Remove the pie weights and foil and return the pastry shell to the oven for 4 minutes to dry the base. Remove from the oven and reduce the oven temperature to 400°F/200°C.

3 Meanwhile, make the filling. Beat the butter and sugar until creamy. Beat in the eggs, one at a time. Add the almonds, flour, orange rind, and almond extract, and beat until blended.

4 Spoon the filling into the pastry shell and smooth the surface. Bake for 30–35 minutes until the top is golden and the tip of a knife inserted in the center comes out clean. Let cool completely on a wire rack, then dust with sifted confectioners' sugar. Serve each slice with a spoonful of sour cream, if desired.

rich chocolate cake

ingredients

SERVES 10–12

- 3 1/2 oz/100 g/generous 1/2 cup raisins
- finely grated rind and juice of 1 orange
- 6 oz/175 g butter, diced, plus extra for greasing
- 3 1/2 oz/100 g semisweet chocolate, at least 70% cocoa solids, broken up
- 4 large eggs, beaten
- 3 1/2 oz/100 g/1/2 cup superfine sugar
- 1 tsp vanilla extract
- 2 oz/55 g/scant 1/2 cup all-purpose flour
- 2 oz/55 g/generous 1/2 cup ground almonds
- 1/2 tsp baking powder
- pinch salt
- 2 oz/55g/scant 1/2 cup blanched almonds, toasted and chopped
- confectioners' sugar, sifted, to decorate

method

1 Put the raisins in a small bowl, add the orange juice, and let soak for 20 minutes. Line a deep 10-inch/25-cm round cake pan with a removable bottom with waxed paper and grease the paper. Set aside.

2 Melt the butter and chocolate together in a small pan over medium heat, stirring. Remove from the heat and set aside to cool.

3 Using an electric mixer, beat the eggs, sugar, and vanilla together for about 3 minutes, until light and fluffy. Stir in the cooled chocolate mixture.

4 Drain the raisins if they haven't absorbed all the orange juice. Sift over the flour, ground almonds, baking powder, and salt. Add the raisins, orange rind, and almonds and fold everything together.

5 Spoon into the cake pan and smooth the surface. Bake in a preheated oven, 350°F/180°C, for about 40 minutes, or until a toothpick inserted into the center comes out clean and the cake starts to come away from the side of the pan. Let cool in the pan for 10 minutes, then remove from the pan and let cool completely on a wire rack. Dust with confectioners' sugar before serving.

lemon tart

ingredients

SERVES 8

10 oz/300 g sweet tart pastry
finely grated rind of 3 lemons
5 fl oz/150 ml/$^2/_3$ cup freshly squeezed lemon juice from 3 or 4 large lemons
3$^1/_2$ oz/100 g/$^1/_2$ cup superfine sugar
5 fl oz/150 ml/$^2/_3$ cup sour cream
3 large eggs, plus 3 large egg yolks
confectioners' sugar, to dust

method

1 Prepare the pastry, roll it out and use to line a 9-inch/23-cm fluted tart pan with a removable base, leaving the excess pastry hanging over the edge. Line the pastry case with a larger piece of waxed paper, then fill with dried beans.

2 Put the lined tart pan on a preheated cookie sheet and bake in a preheated oven, 400°F/ 200°C, for 10–15 minutes, or until the pastry rim looks set. Remove the paper and beans and return the pastry shell to the oven for an additional 5 minutes, or until the bottom looks dry. Remove the pastry shell from the oven, then leave it on the cookie sheet and reduce the oven temperature to 375°F/190°C.

3 Meanwhile, beat the lemon rind, lemon juice, and superfine sugar together until the sugar dissolves. Slowly beat in the sour cream until blended, then beat in the eggs and yolks, one at a time.

4 Carefully pour the filling into the pastry shell, then transfer to the oven and bake for 20–30 minutes, or until the filling is set and the pastry is golden brown. If the pastry, or the filling, looks as though it is becoming too brown, cover the tart with a sheet of foil.

5 Transfer the tart to a cooling rack, then roll a rolling pin over the edge to remove the excess pastry. To serve, remove the pan, and transfer to a serving plate. Dust with confectioners' sugar.

espresso crème brûlée

ingredients

SERVES 4

16 fl oz/450 ml/scant 2 cups heavy cream

1 tbsp instant espresso powder

4 large egg yolks

3½ oz/100 g/½ cup superfine sugar

2 tbsp coffee liqueur

4 tbsp superfine sugar, for glazing

method

1 Place the cream in a small pan over medium-high heat and heat until small bubbles appear around the edges. Mix in the espresso powder, stirring until it dissolves, then remove the pan from the heat and let stand until completely cool.

2 Lightly beat the egg yolks in a bowl, then add the sugar and continue beating until thick and creamy. Reheat the cream over medium-high heat until small bubbles appear around the edges. Stir into the egg-yolk mixture, beating constantly. Stir in the coffee liqueur.

3 Divide the custard mixture among 4 shallow white porcelain dishes placed on a cookie sheet. Bake the custards in a preheated oven, 225°F/110°C, for 35–40 minutes, or until the custard is just 'trembling' when you shake the dishes.

4 Remove the custards from the oven and let cool completely. Cover the surfaces with plastic wrap and let chill in the refrigerator for at least 4 hours, but ideally overnight.

5 Just before you are ready to serve, sprinkle the surface of each custard with the remaining sugar and caramelize with a kitchen blow-torch, or put the dishes under a very hot preheated broiler, until the topping is golden and bubbling. Let cool for a few minutes for the caramel to harden before serving.

spanish caramel custard

ingredients

SERVES 6

18 fl oz/550 ml/scant 2 1/2 cups whole milk
1/2 orange with 2 long, thin pieces of rind removed
1 vanilla bean, split, or 1/2 tsp vanilla extract
6 oz/175 g/scant 1 cup superfine sugar
butter, for greasing the dish
3 large eggs, plus 2 large egg yolks

method

1 Pour the milk into a pan with the orange rind and vanilla bean or extract. Bring to a boil, then remove from the heat and stir in 3 oz/85g/1/2 cup of the sugar; set aside for at least 30 minutes to infuse.

2 Meanwhile, put the remaining sugar and 4 tablespoons of water in another pan over medium-high heat. Stir until the sugar dissolves, then boil without stirring until the caramel turns deep golden brown. Immediately remove the pan from the heat and squeeze in a few drops of orange juice to stop the cooking. Pour into a lightly buttered 40-fl oz/1.25-liter/5-cup soufflé dish and swirl to cover the base; set aside.

3 Return the pan of infused milk to the heat, and bring to a simmer. Beat the whole eggs and egg yolks together in a heatproof bowl. Pour the warm milk into the eggs, whisking constantly. Strain into the soufflé dish.

4 Place the soufflé dish in a roasting pan and pour in enough boiling water to come halfway up the sides of the dish. Bake in a preheated oven, 325°F/160°C, for 75–90 minutes until set and a knife inserted in the center comes out clean. Remove the soufflé dish from the roasting pan and set aside to cool completely. Cover and let chill overnight. To serve, run a metal spatula round the soufflé, then invert onto a serving plate, shaking firmly to release.

pistachio ice cream

ingredients

SERVES 4

10 fl oz/300 ml/1 1/4 cups heavy cream
5 1/2 oz/150 g/2/3 cup strained plain yogurt
2 tbsp milk
3 tbsp Greek honey
green food coloring
1 3/4 oz/50 g/2/3 cup shelled unsalted pistachio nuts, finely chopped

pistachio praline

oil, for brushing
5 1/2 oz/150 g/3/4 cup granulated sugar
3 tbsp water
1 3/4 oz/50 g/2/3 cup shelled, whole, unsalted pistachio nuts

method

1 Set the freezer to its lowest setting. Put the cream, yogurt, milk, and honey in a bowl and mix together. Add a few drops of green food coloring to tint the mixture pale green and stir in well. Pour the mixture into a shallow freezer container and freeze, uncovered, for 1–2 hours, until beginning to set around the edges. Turn the mixture into a bowl and, with a fork, stir until smooth, then stir in the pistachio nuts. Return to the freezer container, cover, and freeze for another 2–3 hours, until firm. Alternatively, use an ice-cream maker, following the manufacturer's instructions.

2 To make the pistachio praline, brush a cookie sheet with oil. Put the sugar and water in a pan and heat gently, stirring, until the sugar has dissolved, then let bubble gently, without stirring, for 6–10 minutes, until lightly golden brown.

3 Remove the pan from the heat and stir in the pistachio nuts. Immediately pour the mixture onto the cookie sheet and spread out evenly. Let stand in a cool place for about 1 hour, until cold and hardened, then put it in a plastic bag and crush with a hammer.

4 About 30 minutes before serving, remove the ice cream from the freezer and let stand at room temperature to soften slightly. To serve, scatter the praline over the ice cream.

sicilian ice cream cake

ingredients

SERVES 4

Genoa sponge cake

6 eggs, separated
7 oz/200 g/1 cup superfine sugar
3 oz/85 g/generous 1/2 cup self-rising flour
3 oz/85 g/generous 1/2 cup cornstarch

filling

1 lb 2 oz/500 g ricotta cheese
7 oz/200 g/1 cup superfine sugar
20 fl oz/625 ml/2 1/2 cups Maraschino liqueur
3 oz/85 g unsweetened chocolate, chopped
7 oz/200 g/generous 1 cup mixed candied peel, diced
10 fl oz/300 ml/1 1/4 cups heavy cream

to decorate

candied cherries, angelica, and citrus fruit, and slivered almonds

method

1 Beat the egg yolks with the sugar until pale and frothy. In a separate, spotlessly clean bowl, whisk the whites until stiff peaks form. Gently fold the whites into the egg yolk mixture with a figure-eight action.

2 Sift the flour and cornstarch into a bowl, then sift into the egg mixture and gently fold in. Pour the mixture into a 10-inch/25-cm cake pan lined with parchment paper, and level the surface. Bake in a preheated oven, 350°F/180°C, for 30 minutes, until springy to the touch. Turn out onto a wire rack, remove the lining paper, and let cool completely.

3 For the filling, combine the ricotta, sugar, and 14 fl oz/425 ml/1 3/4 cups of the Maraschino in a bowl, beating well. Stir in the chopped chocolate and the candied peel.

4 Cut the sponge cake into strips about 1/2 inch/1.25 cm wide and use some of it to line the bottom and sides of a 2-lb/900-g loaf pan. Set aside the remaining slices.

5 Spoon the ricotta mixture into the pan and level the surface. Cover with the reserved sponge cake. Drizzle the remaining Maraschino over the top, then let chill overnight. To serve, turn out onto a serving plate. Whisk the cream until stiff and coat the top and sides of the cake. Decorate with the candied cherries, angelica, and citrus fruit, and the almonds.

lemon sherbet with cava

ingredients

SERVES 4–6

3–4 lemons
9 fl oz/275 ml/scant $1^1/_4$ cups water
7 oz/200 g/1 cup superfine sugar
1 bottle Spanish cava, chilled, to serve

method

1 Roll the lemons on the counter, pressing firmly, which helps to release the juice. Pare off a few strips of rind and set aside for decoration, then finely grate the rind from 3 lemons. Squeeze the juice from as many of the lemons as is necessary to give 6 fl oz/175 ml/$^3/_4$ cup.

2 Put the water and sugar in a heavy-bottom pan over medium-high heat and stir to dissolve the sugar. Bring to a boil, without stirring, and boil for 2 minutes. Remove from the heat, stir in the lemon rind, cover, and let stand for 30 minutes, or until cool.

3 When the mixture is cool, stir in the lemon juice. Strain into an ice-cream maker and freeze according to the manufacturer's instructions. (Alternatively, strain the mixture into a freezerproof container and freeze for 2 hours, or until mushy and freezing round the edges. Tip into a bowl, beat, and return to the freezer. Repeat the process twice more.) 10 minutes before serving, remove the sherbet from the freezer, to soften.

4 To serve, scoop into 4–6 tall glasses, decorate with the reserved rind, if using, and top up with cava.

frozen almond cream with hot chocolate sauce

ingredients

SERVES 4–6

- 6 oz/175 g/generous 1 cup blanched almonds
- 10 fl oz/300 ml/$1^1/_4$ cups heavy cream
- $^1/_4$ tsp almond extract
- 5 fl oz/150 ml/$^2/_3$ cup light cream
- 2 oz/55 g/$^1/_2$ cup confectioners' sugar

hot chocolate sauce

- $3^1/_2$ oz/100 g semisweet chocolate, broken into pieces
- 3 tbsp golden syrup
- 4 tbsp water
- 1 oz/25 g/2 tbsp unsalted butter, diced
- $^1/_4$ tsp vanilla extract

method

1 Toast the almonds on a cookie sheet in a preheated oven, 400°F/200°C, for 7–10 minutes, stirring occasionally, until golden brown. Immediately tip onto a cutting board and let cool. Coarsely chop half the nuts and finely grind the remainder.

2 Whip the heavy cream with the almond extract until soft peaks form. Stir in the light cream and continue whipping, sifting in the sugar in 3 batches. Transfer to an ice-cream maker and freeze. When the cream is almost frozen, transfer it to a bowl, and stir in the chopped almonds. Put the mixture in a 1-lb/450-g loaf pan and smooth the top. Wrap in foil and put in the freezer for at least 3 hours.

3 To make the hot chocolate sauce, place a heatproof bowl over a pan of simmering water. Add the chocolate, syrup, and water and stir until the chocolate melts. Stir in the butter and vanilla extract until smooth.

4 To serve, dip the bottom of the loaf pan in boiling water for a couple of seconds. Invert onto a cutting board, giving a sharp shake to release the frozen cream. Coat the top and sides with the finely chopped almonds. Use a warm knife to slice into 8–12 slices. Arrange two slices on each plate and spoon over the hot chocolate sauce.

mascarpone creams

ingredients

SERVES 4

4 oz/115 g Amaretti cookies, crushed
4 tbsp Amaretto or Maraschino
4 eggs, separated
2 oz/55 g/generous 1/4 cup superfine sugar
8 oz/225 g/1 cup Mascarpone cheese
toasted slivered almonds, to decorate

method

1 Place the Amaretti crumbs in a bowl, add the Amaretto or Maraschino, and set aside to soak.

2 Meanwhile, beat the egg yolks with the superfine sugar until pale and thick. Fold in the Mascarpone and soaked cookie crumbs.

3 Whisk the egg white in a separate, spotlessly clean bowl until stiff, then gently fold into the cheese mixture. Divide the Mascarpone cream among 4 serving dishes and let chill for 1–2 hours. Sprinkle with toasted slivered almonds just before serving.

creamy chocolate dessert

ingredients

SERVES 4–6

6 oz/175 g semisweet chocolate, at least 70% cocoa solids, broken up
1½ tbsp orange juice
3 tbsp water
2 tbsp unsalted butter, diced
2 eggs, separated
⅛ tsp cream of tartar
3 tbsp superfine sugar
6 tbsp heavy cream

pistachio-orange praline

corn oil, for greasing
2 oz/55 g/generous ¼ cup superfine sugar
2 oz/55 g/scant ½ cup shelled pistachios
finely grated rind of 1 large orange

method

1 Melt the chocolate with the orange juice and water in a small pan over very low heat, stirring constantly. Remove from the heat, add the butter, stirring until incorporated. Using a rubber spatula, scrape the chocolate into a bowl. Beat the egg yolks, then beat them into the chocolate mixture. Set aside to cool.

2 In a clean bowl, whisk the egg whites with the cream of tartar until soft peaks form. Gradually beat in the sugar, 1 tablespoon at a time, beating well after each addition, until the meringue is glossy. Beat 1 tablespoon of the meringue mixture into the chocolate mixture, then fold in the rest.

3 In a separate bowl, whip the cream until soft peaks form. Fold into the chocolate mixture. Spoon into individual glass bowls or wine glasses, or 1 large serving bowl. Cover with plastic wrap and let chill for at least 4 hours.

4 To make the praline, lightly grease a cookie sheet with corn oil and set aside. Put the sugar and pistachios in a small pan over medium heat. When the sugar starts to melt, stir gently until a liquid caramel forms and the nuts start popping. Pour the praline onto the cookie sheet and immediately finely grate the orange rind over. Let cool until firm then coarsely chop. Just before serving, sprinkle the praline over the chocolate pudding.

chocolate & cherry tiramisù

ingredients

SERVES 4

- 7 fl oz/200 ml/generous 3/4 cup strong black coffee, cooled to room temperature
- 6 tbsp cherry brandy
- 16 trifle sponges
- 9 oz/250 g/1 1/4 cups Mascarpone
- 10 fl oz/300 ml/1 1/4 cups heavy cream, lightly whipped
- 3 tbsp confectioner's sugar
- 9 1/2 oz/275 g sweet cherries, halved and pitted
- 2 1/4 oz/60 g chocolate, curls or grated
- whole cherries, to decorate

method

1 Pour the cooled coffee into a pitcher and stir in the cherry brandy. Put half of the trifle sponges into the bottom of a serving dish, then pour over half of the coffee mixture.

2 Put the Mascarpone into a separate bowl along with the cream and sugar, and mix well. Spread half of the Mascarpone mixture over the coffee-soaked trifle sponges, then top with half of the cherries. Arrange the remaining trifle sponges on top. Pour over the remaining coffee mixture and top with the remaining cherries. Finish with a layer of Mascarpone mixture. Scatter over the chocolate curls, cover with plastic wrap, and let chill in the refrigerator for at least 2 hours.

3 Remove from the refrigerator, decorate with whole cherries, and serve.

broiled honey figs with zabaglione

ingredients

SERVES 4

8 fresh figs, cut in half

4 tbsp honey

2 fresh rosemary sprigs, leaves removed and finely chopped (optional)

3 eggs

method

1 Preheat the broiler to high. Arrange the figs, cut-side up, on the broiler pan. Brush with half the honey and sprinkle over the rosemary, if using.

2 Cook under the preheated broiler for 5–6 minutes, or until just starting to caramelize.

3 Meanwhile, to make the zabaglione, lightly whisk the eggs with the remaining honey in a large, heatproof bowl, then place over a pan of simmering water. Using a hand-held electric whisk, beat the eggs and honey for 10 minutes, or until pale and thick.

4 Put 4 fig halves on each of 4 serving plates, add a generous spoonful of the zabaglione, and serve at once.

baked apricots with honey

ingredients

SERVES 4

butter, for greasing
4 apricots, each cut in half and pitted
4 tbsp slivered almonds
4 tbsp honey
pinch ground ginger or grated nutmeg
vanilla ice cream, to serve (optional)

method

1 Lightly butter an ovenproof dish large enough to hold the apricot halves in a single layer.

2 Arrange the apricot halves in the dish, cut sides up. Sprinkle with the almonds and drizzle the honey over. Dust with the spice.

3 Bake in a preheated oven, 400°F/200°C, for 12–15 minutes until the apricots are tender and the almonds golden. Remove from the oven and serve at once, with ice cream on the side, if desired.

marsala cherries

ingredients

SERVES 4

5 oz/140 g/generous 1/2 cup superfine sugar
thinly pared rind of 1 lemon
2-in/5-cm piece of cinnamon stick
8 fl oz/250 ml/1 cup water
8 fl oz/250 ml/1 cup Marsala
2 lb /900 g Morello cherries, pitted
5 fl oz/150 ml/2/3 cup heavy cream

method

1 Put the sugar, lemon rind, cinnamon stick, water, and Marsala in a heavy-bottom pan and bring to a boil, stirring constantly. Reduce the heat and let simmer for 5 minutes. Remove the cinnamon stick.

2 Add the Morello cherries, cover, and let simmer gently for 10 minutes. Using a slotted spoon, transfer the cherries to a bowl.

3 Return the pan to the heat and bring to a boil over high heat. Boil for 3–4 minutes, until thick and syrupy. Pour the syrup over the cherries and set aside to cool, then chill for at least 1 hour.

4 Whisk the cream until stiff peaks form. Divide the cherries and syrup among 4 individual dishes or glasses, top with the cream, and serve.